150 Lessons Learned from
50 Years in Consulting

150 Lessons Learned from 50 Years in Consulting

Thomas L. Greenbaum

Founder, ENCORE Strategic
Business Consulting

Copyright

Disclaimer

Dedication

This book is dedicated to all the people who have contributed to my success in the consulting business over the past 45+ years... You know who you are.

It is also dedicated to my wife and partner for 55+ years, who has always been both my inspiration and my greatest supporter.

Finally, I dedicate the book to my very best friend, my brother Allie who has been a source of fun, family, and frolic for my entire life. I am so lucky to have had such a close relationship with him for the past 78+ years.

Excellence is never an accident. It is always the result of high intention, sincere effort, and intelligent execution; it represents the wise choice of many alternatives—choice, not chance, determines your destiny.
— Aristotle

Other Books by
Thomas Greenbaum

The Practical Handbook and Guide to Focus Group Research (1986). Lexington Books

The Consultant's Manual (1990) John Wiley & Sons
(A complete Guide to Building a Successful Consulting Practice)

The Handbook for Focus Group Research (1993) Lexington Books

The Handbook for Focus Group Research - Second Edition. (1998) Sage Publications

Moderating Focus Groups (2000) Sage Publications

You Can Do It: A Guide to Starting and Running a Small Business. (2012). 72nd St Books

You Can Do it: A Guide to Starting and Running a Small Business – 2018 Edition (2018). 72nd St. Books

Table of Contents

Introduction

I lied! Actually, I have only been in the consulting industry for 48 years, but it would not have been as appealing a title. However, perhaps I can be excused from this little white lie because there are more than 150 lessons included in this book.

Several people have asked why I decided to write this book. Almost two years ago, after finishing my seventh book, *You Can Do It; A Guide to Starting and Running a Small Business*, I promised myself and my family that that was my last literary effort. While I really enjoy the process of putting ideas on paper if they will be helpful to others, going through the process of writing a book is very time-consuming and stressful. However, despite my real intention to never do another book, when I came up with the idea for this one, I could not resist. It sort of summarizes the ideas and lessons of all my other books into a very short but information-intensive manuscript.

I have always been the type of individual who enjoys helping people, whether it is related to business or personal issues. To this end, over the past 47+ years, I spent 11 years working for an organization called SCORE (Service Corps for Retired Executives), where I worked 20-40 hours per week mentoring with small and medium-size businesses for FREE, just so I could help businesspeople who could not afford to retain outside consulting assistance. Helping these people was very rewarding, both from the perspective of seeing their businesses grow or stopping them from investing in a bad idea, but as with almost every consulting assignment I completed, my biggest reward was the learning I got from working with the clients. I can say without reservation that I learned as much from the 1000+ clients I worked with at SCORE as, hopefully, they did from me.

As I will detail in the next chapter of this book, I have been fortunate to consult with clients in a very wide range of areas ranging from very high-level issues relating to corporate management in Fortune 500 companies to almost every aspect of both profit and nonprofit entities in the areas of marketing, sales, marketing research, and new product development, just to name a few in very small organizations, both profit and nonprofit. Each of the lessons I learned has contributed to my knowledge and experience base that has enabled me to be an effective consultant for my clients for almost one-half century. It would be my greatest pleasure if others could benefit from the lessons described in this book. To this end, I would love to hear from readers as to whether they got some good lessons from this book that improved the performance in their careers

Thomas L. Greenbaum
New York City
2021

Organization of the Book

My goal in writing this book was to make it an easy-to-use reference book for anyone involved in a business, whether it is a Fortune 100 company, a one-person consulting practice, or the manager of a retail bookstore. The content has been divided into sections based on discrete areas of management, so it is easy to find specific information that is of particular interest to my readers. For each lesson, I have tried to develop a memorable headline idea, with the explanation of the lesson covered in the subsequent text.

The first chapter of the book provides an overview of my career both in the corporate world and, more importantly, in the various consulting positions I have had over the past 40+ years. My goal is to demonstrate how the various jobs contributed to the 150+ lessons I have learned.

I would love to hear comments from readers about the various lessons that are discussed in this book, as I am very interested in learning which ones were most helpful.

Chapter One
My Career in Consulting

A book such as this would not have nearly as much meaning without providing some information about how all the lessons were learned. Therefore, the objective of this chapter is to provide a brief overview of the various types of consulting positions I have had over the past 47+ years. Each of the positions I have had added different types of lessons primarily because of the nature of the clientele for whom I have worked and the wide variety of areas in which I have had to become involved.

Life in Business Before Consulting

As I look back on my career, I feel that I was extremely lucky in the choices I made, as they were integral to providing me with the training and experiences necessary to be an effective consultant. My first job, after I graduated from Columbia Business School (MBA), was with Procter & Gamble (P&G) in Cincinnati. There is no question in my mind that this was the most important job choice I ever made, as in 1966, when I went to P&G, it was generally regarded to be the best company in the world to learn about the field of marketing. This was true, but even more importantly, my work in the Paper Products Division at P&G taught me how to write and think as a business leader. While it was a very painful experience, due to the challenges your superiors would place in front of you, the discipline I learned at P&G

5

has been the key to my success in the consulting business. At P&G, you learn how marketing should be done and what processes and practices you should employ to analyze and solve problems. Also, P&G provided me with real-world sales experience in the grocery industry, which has proved to be vital as I worked with clients in sales-related assignments.

In the middle of my P&G career, I had to leave for 731 days (but who was counting) to complete my ROTC commitment to the U.S. Army Infantry. I spent all my time at Ft. Benning, GA, despite the fact that everyone else in my 234-person officer basic training unit was shipped to (mostly) unpleasant places like Viet Nam. My two years at Ft. Benning also were great training for my ultimate career in consulting as I was assigned to a general staff as a member of the Infantry School budget office. I was lucky to be exposed to both formal schooling (Ft. Benjamin Harrison School of Finance) and practical use of special training in government finance. However, the most important part of my work at Ft. Benning was my responsibility to do extensive writing in response to immediate requests from the Commanding General about topics such as the financial impact of issues such as doubling the output of the OCS (Overseas Communication Service) program, the airborne school or the Army Ranger program. Further, my job required me to brief high-ranking generals from all parts of our military regarding the cost and management implications of the issues we were asked to evaluate. Speaking to groups like this was excellent training for my life as a consultant, as public speaking has never been an issue with me after all my experiences as an army officer in the high-pressure environment of the U.S. Army Infantry School.

After leaving the military, I returned to Procter & Gamble for two years and continued to grow as a result of their hardcore training needed to fit into the mold of disciplined marketing experts. A key part of my lessons learned upon returning to P&G after the army was the very intense sales training I received while working in my territory in the Cincinnati Region.

After 2+ years again at P&G, I left to become a product manager and then a group product manager at what was then a very small company ($16 million in sales) known as Church and Dwight. When I joined that company, they basically had three products. One was Arm & Hammer Baking Soda, which accounted for almost all company revenue and profits, and the others were Arm & Hammer Washing Soda and Arm & Hammer Borax. While at Arm & Hammer, I was assigned the task of introducing Arm & Hammer Laundry Detergent into the United States. Also, I was tasked with talking to inventors to attempt to identify viable new product opportunities for the company that would expand the product line further.

There were so many important lessons from the two years I spent at Church & Dwight. Whereas at P&G, I felt that I learned how to do everything the right way, I always felt that at Church & Dwight, I learned how the rest of the world viewed marketing. Church & Dwight did not have the same discipline or attention to detail as P&G, nor did they have the focus on emphasizing training and development of the employees, but I did have some very unusual experiences. For example, the experience of introducing a major new product in a highly competitive product category (laundry category) was very growth-producing both in terms of learning what to do and what not to do with a new product introduction. I also learned the challenges associated with managing a food broker sales organization rather than working with a direct sales organization, as was the case at P&G. Both of these were vital to the experiences needed to be an effective consultant.

On To Consulting

Exactly two years after I joined Church & Dwight, I had the opportunity to join a very successful consulting company called Glendinning Associates. This was a consulting organization that was staffed almost exclusively by former P&G marketing or sales personnel, many of whom had made an intermediate career stop somewhere else to gain some varied experience. The "reason why" of the Glendinning organization was that its staff of P&G trained consultants would impart the knowledge and practical experience learned at Procter (as it is affectionately called) to improve the marketing and sales effectiveness of our clients. Most of the companies with whom we consulted were very major organizations, giving me the experience of working with internationally known names like Lever Brothers, The Wrigley Company, Ralston Purina, and The Bank of Montreal, just to name a few. One of the things I did not learn at Glendinning Associates was how to work with very small companies, which was a major part of my career several years later when I worked for SCORE.

Following almost eight years at Glendinning Associates, four other colleagues and I left and formed The Connecticut Consulting Group. Four of us were former P&G marketing or salespeople, and one was a veteran of General Foods, the other great marketing training company at that time. This was another great situation to learn even more about how to work with large companies, but also it gave me the experience of a partnership where five equal partners had to work out the strategies and logistics to run an effective consulting practice. I learned how partnerships should and should not work and how important it is to have strong partnership agreements when you stake your career on the efforts of yourself and others.

After seven years building The Connecticut Consulting Group to be a large and profitable consulting practice, we had the opportunity to sell our organization to what was then D'Arcy McManus Benton & Bowles, which eventually became Publicis. The process of selling our company was one of the most important lessons I learned, which would prove to be very helpful to my clients in future years as they dealt with the opportunity to sell their company or buy another.

The sale of the Connecticut Consulting Group actually started me on another consulting career that was vital to my "lessons learned" up until the current time. While I continued to consult with large corporate clients, in 1986, I wrote my first book, *The Practical Handbook and Guide to Focus Group Research*, which enabled me to migrate from large company strategic consulting to the market research business, specifically conducting focus groups. My new career (focus groups) was supported by our new company and enabled me to be a specialist in this much larger marketing agency and consulting practice. Focus group research was the primary consulting work in which I was involved during the four years I spent with Clarion Marketing & Consulting, the new name for our consulting company resulting from the merger of the Connecticut Consulting Group and Ted Colangelo Associates which was then a D'Arcy subsidiary.

In 1993, I departed Clarion and started my own focus group company, Groups Plus, Inc., doing essentially the same type of market research projects that I was doing while part of Clarion. An important "lesson" I learned very quickly from my work in the market research field was that the industry had almost no one who was a qualified focus group moderator and also an experienced strategic business consultant. As a result, I had a very strong point of difference between myself and almost everyone else in the business, which was the key to my being able to obtain clients representing both large and small organizations. In my role as focus group moderator and marketing consultant, I was able to conduct the research to explore their research needs, AND importantly use my experience to recommend what specific actions they should take as a result of the findings and conclusions from the research. I conducted almost 4000 focus groups with over 300 different organizations during my time as President of Groups Plus, Inc.

In 2009 I started a completely new phase of my consulting career, which produced the most important lessons of my career relating to starting and running a business. Although I had run my own business for 15 years, it was not until I had spent about five years at SCORE (Service Corps of Retired Executives) that I felt I was sufficiently skilled to help small businesses. I worked as a volunteer counselor for 11 years at SCORE, counseling with approximately 1100 different SMALL BUSINESS clients, helping them in all aspects of their business, including such areas as organization startup/corporate form, fundraising, marketing, sales, and importantly, the whole area of social media and web site development and operation. The type of clientele we serviced consisted mostly of 1–2-person organizations who wanted to start a business or get help managing one that already existed. With this type of counseling/consulting, you can really make a major difference in an organization in terms of whether they become successful or not. The following are three examples of success stories from my years at SCORE (written without names for confidentiality) that were key lessons learned by me, which have been reflected in this book.

CASE #1

I worked with a client that appeared to have a very successful company in terms of total dollar sales and sales growth, but the owners were unhappy because they never had enough money in their bank to generate income for themselves, which was consistent with the sales revenue. After an analysis of the organization, I learned that while the sales were very strong, the weakness of the company was they were not successfully collecting the money they were owed, so their outstanding receivables were almost equal to their sales. While the reader of this might suggest that the owners were dumb and this was unusual, I can say that probably the most common problem I saw with small companies was their lack of attention to their receivables. If you do not collect the money due to you from sales, the "sale" has not been successful. Thus, I learned a very important lesson that has been shared with scores of clients over the years.

CASE #2

Another example of a great lesson learned was a company that came to me during their first few years in business, with the complaint that they were not growing and could not see a viable future that might generate a meaningful income for the two partners. The company had two very smart, competent owners who were teaching swimming to a very specific group of challenged children. The main issue/lesson learned with this client was that the only way for them to grow was to work more hours every week. They did not understand the concept of leverage in terms of training people who do what they did, so it was possible to expand the services to other places, thus generating more income.

The most important contribution we made to this organization was to convince the two principles to reduce their time in the pool so the employees could do most of the teaching while they focused on expanding to other cities where they could hire more people to teach using their methods. Further, they learned about the importance of supervising their employees, so they were diligent in following the teaching methods they had developed. It is very common for the leader(s) of entrepreneurial companies to feel they must do all the work because (a) nobody can do it as good as they can, and (b) if they are not doing the work, they don't feel they are making money for the company.

I have seen this exact same behavior while working with people in the legal profession, medical profession, and the retail store category. It is an important lesson, but the key to a successful business is to use leverage in the organization by hiring others to do work for you while you focus on building the sales of the total

11

organization. Another key lesson from this case was learning that the time spent training someone to do the work would pay out in multiples rather than the owner feeling that he or she must do all the work to be successful.

CASE #3

Another example of where experiences with clients have generated important lessons learned was the work I was involved in with a toy start-up company. This client came to me after having won numerous awards for the quality of their toys, and they even were successful in getting a major piece on the TODAY show. Still, they were not succeeding, despite the great product and wonderful public relations activity. Their sales were a fraction of what they had projected. Interestingly, this client had written a very extensive business plan which won a major award sponsored by one of the leading MBA programs in the country. The owners simply could not understand what was wrong.

With this client, the major problem was a lack of understanding of their target customer's buying habits. As a result, they were focused on selling their products using sales channels that were not optimal for this product. After analyzing their business and the product category in order to understand the buying behavior of their target audience, we learned that their customers bought the vast majority of this product category in traditional brick and mortar retail stores rather than online, which was the focus of their marketing plan. Once the sales strategy was changed to a retail store model, the company flourished, even getting distribution in stores such as Toys 'R' Us and FAO Schwarz.

After 11 years in the SCORE organization, I got tired of volunteering my time for 20-40 hours per week, and I retired from this nonprofit to go back to my roots as a strategic business consultant. My new consulting company, ENCORE Strategic Business

Consulting, was started in November 2019, and as of this writing, it has been a very successful venture for me. I have worked pro bono for a couple of needed organizations, but more importantly, have had 3-4 fee-paying clients which whom I have been working regularly doing the type of consulting I have done all my life, applying lessons learned from many years in the business to my current clients.

The balance of this book contains the lessons laid out in a format that I hope will be helpful to many people who read this book. I have enjoyed writing it (as I have all my other books) and only hope it achieves my objective of HELPING businesspeople succeed in their business careers.

Chapter Two
Lessons

Marketing Lessons

1) **Never change the composition of a product in order to save money.** It is not uncommon for an organization to try and increase the profitability of a successful product by changing some ingredients that are less expensive than what is currently in the formula. The thought is that if these changes are made, the consumer will not know the difference, and the product will contribute more profit to the organization. Based on my experience, eventually, the consumers will recognize the differences, and the brand franchise will begin to decline.

Perhaps the most famous example of this was the introduction of the *new Coke* in 1985. While there are many reasons why this was one of history's most famous marketing failures, the primary motivation for this was the need to improve the financial structure of the company. A few years earlier, they had replaced sugar with corn fructose, a much less expensive sweetener, and they experienced a significant market share decline to Pepsi Cola. As a result of this, the Coke chairman, Mr. Giunta, felt a new, more profitable Coke would turn the situation around and restore the brand to its former market share. As everyone knows, the *new Coke* brand lasted only a very short time, and Coke did not restore its earnings position until *Diet Coke* became the #3 brand in the world behind Coke and Pepsi in the late 1980s.

Another example of this to which almost everyone can relate to frequently occurs in the restaurant industry. A new restaurant opens to great reviews, and it is almost impossible to get a reservation. As a result of this success, it is not uncommon for the restaurant to try and cut costs by eliminating some amenities they had during the early years (i.e., desert candies, complementary after-dinner drinks, an amuse-bouche at the beginning of the meal, or even the quality of the bread that is served. In relatively short order, the restaurant loses some of its allure, and they start to wonder why.

2) **You cannot spend too much time or money on efforts to understand your customers.** The more you know about the behavior and attitudes of your customers, the better able you will be to develop advertising copy, promotional ideas, and sales programs to effectively market to this group. Further, by regularly evaluating attitudes toward the product or service, you will know when the optimal time is to make changes that the customer would prefer. One of the best "investments" organizations can make is to learn about their customers and prospects, and this should be an ongoing effort. Most of the well-known companies with sophisticated marketing personnel will regularly check in with their audience to understand changes in attitudes within the product category or concerning the products being evaluated.

3) **The most important word in all of marketing is BENE-FIT.** For years I have been talking to my clients about thinking of their marketing efforts from the perspective of the customer in terms of "what's in it for me?" Most organizations,

16

and particularly service companies, utilize external communications (i.e., advertising, social media, website copy, etc.) that focus on them and what they offer to customers. It is rare that I run into an organization that looks at their communications from the customer point of view. To this end, I really believe that almost all purchase decisions, whether in the retail, governmental or industrial sectors are ultimately about what is in it for me... the BENEFIT. For example, will this purchase make me look good to my boss, will this electric drill make it easier for me to do my hobby or job, will this new shirt make me look handsome? I was recently working with a client on their website, and I realized that the entire site was focused on telling prospective clients all the great things they have to offer and all the extensive experience they have in different product categories. However, they had absolutely nothing that communicated the real BENEFITS to their customer of hiring their company. If the readers of this book remember only one thing, it should be the importance of focusing all their efforts on the BENEFITS for their customers rather than internally focusing on what they have to offer.

4) **It is essential that marketing personnel understand and apply the concept of INVESTMENT SPENDING.** The essence of this concept is that money spent on marketing programs should focus on the return it will develop over time rather than be considered an expense. Investment spending is particularly relevant to the introduction of new products, in which case the amount of money spent during the initial 6-12 months of the life of the new product or service is focused on building awareness and trial, which are the two most important outcomes of a product or service introduction. To this end, the amount of money spent during the early years in the life of the venture probably will not generate a profitable venture at that point in time, but rather they are an investment in building a franchise

for the product or service. As most people would consider with financial investments, it is important to recognize that the return from an investment may not be immediate, but if utilized properly, it will pay off in the near future.

5) **When trying to build the revenues and profits of a service business, one of the most important avenues to pursue is *prior customers*.** It is so common for a service company to spend huge amounts of money to find new clients/customers for their business, yet they often forget to aim their marketing efforts at prior clients where they had a successful relationship. Prior clients/customers are ideal as they are already familiar with your organization and both the type and quality of work you will do for them. They should have an appreciation for the BENEFITS you offer without you having to sell them on how you could be helpful. Further, you will almost always know multiple personnel in the prior client organization, and you should have an in-depth understanding of their business. You can merchandise how this prior work experience with them will help you quickly get up to speed on what you need to learn about their existing problem or opportunity, and therefore you will be able to become effective for them much quicker than another organization.

6) **A very important concept for marketers to understand is that the *"product is hero."*** The essence of this concept is that when advertising a particular brand, the focus of the ad should be on the product or service that is advertised. Very often, we see advertising where it is difficult to understand what product or service is being promoted. I have also seen this in brand and corporate logos, where there is so much extraneous material that it is very difficult to determine what the name of the product or service is that should be communicated. The best way to demonstrate the importance of this concept is to watch a television program,

and at the end, try and remember the products that were advertised. This concept applies to traditional advertising, Internet advertising, packaging, and all other external communications vehicles employed to market the product or service.

7) **The more single-minded your marketing message, the better the communication will be in terms of target customer comprehension and recall.** It is a very common practice of marketing personnel to try to include several different copy points in an external communication such as an advertisement, promotion, email campaign, web ad, or another type of vehicle. However, the more the communication can focus on one key copy point (benefit!), the greater the chance the target consumer will recall this message and perhaps even act on it.

8) **For years we have been advising clients NOT to utilize cursive (script) or very stylized fonts in logos, names, signage, or advertising.** Unless you have the budget of a brand such as Coca-Cola and are willing to invest many years into developing awareness of your communication, refrain from using cursive or any fancy fonts. They simply are much more difficult to read than a more standard font, thus making the job of building name or brand awareness much more difficult.

9) **One of the most fundamental lessons learned about advertising communications is that the *words and pictures* must go together.** While this seems so obvious to the experienced marketeer, it is so often violated, thus dramatically reducing the effectiveness of the communication. Consumer's people will dramatically improve their comprehension and recall of any commercial vehicle if what they see in a visual is essentially what they hear or read.

10) **A very short slogan/tag line which becomes a part of a brand name and logo will dramatically increase the consumer understanding of your brand or corporate identity.** The prototypical example I have used for years is the BMW logo, which you always see with the words "the ultimate driving machine." By having the words as part of the name and logo, you not only communicate what the product (or service) is, but you can and should also deliver a BENEFIT in the slogan. In this case, the benefit is the superiority of the automobile. This lesson becomes even more important when dealing with a name that does not have the recognition of an entity such as BMW. For example, if you are starting a consulting company called Smith Consulting, you can create a very unique logo to go along with the name, but you still have not communicated what Smith does and why the target consumer should hire this organization. However, if under the name Smith Consulting (whether or not they choose to have a unique logo) you included the words "Web development services with a 100% satisfaction guarantee," the person that sees the name would clearly know that Smith develops websites, and the benefit is that you will have a guarantee of money back if you are not satisfied.

11) **The concept of product (or service) *positioning* is a lesson that I learned many years ago, and it has enabled me to help hundreds of clients establish the most promising marketing programs for their products or services.** Positioning is a concept that was made popular by two advertising executives (Trout & Reis) in the early 1960s in a fantastic book they wrote called *Positioning, The Battle for Your Mind*. This book has been updated since that time, but the basic concept of positioning they formalized has not. Essentially, positioning is the concept of what you want your target customers to think about when they see your name or think about your product or service. It really

should be the starting point for all marketing programs, as every element of the marketing mix should be oriented around building awareness of and understanding of the position your product or service has in the marketplace. It is the niche in which you operate and the "handle" you have that makes you different from everyone else in your competitive space. Some examples of positioning that are well known are Diet Coke (Just for the taste of it), Apple (Think Different), Bounty Towels (The Quicker Picker Upper), McDonald's (I'm Lovin' It), and Dunkin' Donuts (America Runs on Dunkin'). The key to a good *position* is that it is unique to your product or service, communicates a BENEFIT to the consumer, and could not be used by any other brand since it is too strongly tied to your name/ identity.

12) **One of the most important lessons I have learned as a consultant has morphed into the image of a *three-legged stool*, with specific elements of the stool representing different aspects of the overall concept.** The purpose of the stool graphic is to demonstrate how a service organization can generate awareness among its target audience without spending significant money in advertising or marketing. This *STOOL* graphic/concept is such an important lesson in marketing that I devoted an entire chapter to it in my most recent book, *You Can Do It; A Guide to Starting and Running a Small Business.* The entire focus of the stool is the identification of a specific action that a service organization can take to generate awareness without spending money.

The seat of the stool represents *awareness,* which is the most important marketing result for any organization as, if nobody knows who you are, it is impossible to generate sales. Each of the legs of the stool has a letter, either S, W, or N. The "S" stands for *speaking,* indicating the importance of giving speeches or presentations to key groups of your target audience about your area of expertise that demonstrates the BENEFITS you provide your clients. The "W" stands for the importance of *writing,* to help you generate awareness by the use of a variety of written vehicles, such as blogging, writing articles for publication, having articles written about your company, or writing a book about your area of expertise. One thing I can say for sure is that if you can write a good book, you will find this is one of the best ways to build both awareness and credibility that you can ever implement. My first book in 1986, *The Practical Handbook and Guide to Focus Group Research,* started an entirely new career for me as a sub-segment of my work in marketing. The final leg of the stool is the "N," which stands for *networking.* The principle behind networking is the concept of keeping in regular touch with as many individuals as possible who might possibly be a source of business or a referral to you as a potential source of business. This can be accomplished by belonging to a formal networking organization, of which there are many, or just maintaining an active posture of communicating via letter, email, phone, or personal contact with as many people as possible who meet the standards identified previously.

13) **It is essential that once a brand identity has been established, the organization should be rigid about adherence to the "look," not varying any element without an extremely good reason.** This is the essence of *brand identity,* one of the most well-recognized marketing "must-haves." I have experienced client organizations that did not adhere to strict identity standards and used 3-5 different logos in the market at the same time. With more than one "look," it is extremely difficult to develop a meaningful level of awareness of what the company stands for as manifested by whatever brand identity has been developed.

14) Even though we currently operate in a very high-tech environment where almost everything is electronic, I strongly urge service organizations to develop a trifold paper *brochure* for their organization. A trifold brochure is a document that accomplishes three very important things for an organization. First, it forces the identification of the key strengths and limitations of the organization and, more importantly, the most significant BENEFITS that you can offer to clients. Secondly, it provides the organization with a very effective sales tool that can work as an intermediary between initial personal, telephonic or internet contact, and the company website. Third, it also is a most effective "leave-behind" when giving a speech or after a face-to-face meeting. The size of the ideal trifold brochure should be a single sheet of 8½" by 11" paper, then folded to a trifold. Detailed instructions covering what information should be presented in a trifold brochure are provided in my book, *You Can Do It; A Guide to Starting and Running a Small Business* – Revised 2018 Edition.

Management Lessons

1) **Things are never as good or as bad as they seem at any given time.** In the business world, it is very easy to get overly excited about an accomplishment, a deal you have made, or a very positive review from your boss. Similarly, we all make mistakes that can cause problems. You write a bad recommendation or get a bad review from a superior, a client, or an outside reviewer looking at your material. What I have been telling clients for years is that how you feel at the current time should not be viewed as a permanent state. Things change as time passes, and if you can accept the premise that situations always appear to be better or worse than they really are at the moment, as time passes, you will get through this situation. The practical lesson here is to enjoy your successes but don't think that is a permanent state, and also, if things go bad, they are not forever, and things will change.

2) **Very often, an "atta-boy" can be as effective as a monetary bonus.** All of us need validation for the work we do by the people in our work environment. It is relatively easy to give someone a monetary bonus for something they did well, but my experience clearly shows that the permanent impact of a bonus can be short-lived. However, recognition of your accomplishment by someone whose opinion is of value, such as a client, a boss, or perhaps a peer, can have a very long-lasting impact on the morale and ultimate performance of the individual.

3) **Think with your head and not your heart.** The essence of this lesson is to do what is best for your business rather than what will necessarily make you feel better. A common

example of this, which I have personally experienced, is to retain an employee for a time far beyond their usefulness to the organization, just because they have been around a long time or because you just happen to really like the person. This mistake once cost me almost $200,000 and was the difference between a profit and loss for the business over a 3-year period. It is very difficult to take emotion out of business decisions, but if you can keep the "think with your head and not your heart" phrase in the back of your mind, I am confident you will make much better decisions over time.

4) **If your business is growing rapidly, hire ahead of the growth.** It is very rewarding (emotionally and financially) to have a successful business that is growing rapidly. The point in time when you are confident that your business will continue to grow is the precise time to hire for future needs, rather than wait until you achieve the next level of your growth spurt and then need to quickly find the right person to fill the position you need. A common example of this is a successful consulting practice, where the senior people are working crazy hours because of all the work that they have generated and recognize that it must be completed on the agreed-upon timetable. If the leaders had determined that the growth they are experiencing seems to be a trend, then they should have identified the right time to hire the people that are needed to enable the company to continue to grow without placing undue pressures on the limited staff that is currently available to handle the workload.

5) **Micromanaging is a major sign of management weakness and is not an effective way to work.** Some managers just cannot trust anyone else to do the work that has to be accomplished, so they feel compelled to oversee every detail of everything their subordinates do. While the end

result of some projects might be better because of the micromanagement, this practice is very counter-productive. It does not contribute to the training of your employees, and it can be the cause of a major morale problem among the staff who probably feel you do not trust them to do quality work. Further, as the manager is getting caught up in the "weeds" of every project done by the staff, it is almost impossible to develop the overall strategic perspective that is necessary to provide the leadership which will give your organization the best possible chance of success.

6) **Invest in training your staff, even if it is much less productive in the short term.** As a manager, there are many times when you receive a work product from a subordinate and your knee-jerk reaction is to redo it yourself, as it will get done quicker and will have a better result. As a manager (and a consultant), I have experienced this many times. It might only be a short letter to a client or an internal email to another person in the company, but if you do it rather than take the time to work with your staff (or your clients) so they can learn how to do it correctly, you will never be happy with the output of your staff. It is worthwhile to remember that "you can give him a fish and feed him for a day, or teach him how to fish and feed him for a lifetime." As a junior person at Procter & Gamble, and even as a new consultant at Glendinning Associates, I was asked to rewrite documents often, sometimes as many as 8-10 versions. While I found this very frustrating and extremely annoying, it really is the best way to learn to think and write effectively. My superiors always knew they could have completed the job much faster, but if I had not gone through this "redo" process, I would have never learned how to do it correctly, so I could be a more effective and ultimately efficient contributor to the organization. So, the time spent teaching your subordinates or clients to do the task well will pay out in multiples in the future.

7) **One of the most effective keys to managing your time and that of your subordinates is to utilize *project lists.*** Simply defined, a project list is a compilation of the various tasks you have to accomplish, listed by the due date. I have always advised my clients to have their personnel develop project lists that are updated weekly relative to priorities and due dates. If these are provided to the superior for review and comment, the supervisor can be on top of what the individual is doing, and the subordinate has no question regarding the priorities associated with the work. While this appears to be a very fundamental tool, most clients I have worked with do not require this of themselves or their personnel. The lists are also a great tool to learn why some tasks do not get completed and to provide leadership and direction to subordinates to help them solve a problem that may have been hindering their performance.

8) **The keys to running an effective meeting are to start on time and to have a written agenda.** One of the biggest complaints I hear from client personnel is the time they waste in meetings. This is often caused by not starting the meeting on time and/or not having a clear picture of why this meeting has been called and what topics are to be covered. A manager that gets a reputation for always starting meetings on time will find out very quickly that people coming to his or her meeting will come on time because they understand that is the expectation, and if they are not there, it will be noticed by everyone, and they will be missing the information transmitted before they arrived. Further, by starting (and ending) on time, it shows respect for the value of the time of others.

A meeting without an agenda can often go way off on tangents and waste precious time, covering topics that are not as important or relevant as those for which the meeting has been called. Attendees to a meeting always feel better when they can see (in writing) the purpose of the meeting and what topics will be covered. Also, if an agenda is distributed prior to the meeting, the attendees will be much better prepared for the topics to be discussed.

9) **It is almost impossible to do too much planning.** While most people in management will nod their heads aggressively when talking about the benefits of planning, there is a very good chance that they really do very little of it. Organizations that operate without a long-term strategic plan and appropriate annual plans are much less likely to succeed than those that make a commitment to a formal planning process. In its most basic form, a plan is nothing more than a roadmap with a target destination.

Prior to the advent of the GPS systems, no one would start a long road trip without getting a map and marking the route from start to finish. That is essentially what a business plan will do. It provides a target for the organization and the activities that will be implemented in order to accomplish the plan. Occasionally organizations get very hung-up with the most appropriate format for a business or marketing plan. My personal view is that the content of the plan is much more important than the format. While I have my own ideas about the format for business plans for both large and small companies (outlined in my book, *You Can Do It: A Guide to Starting and Running a Small Business),* I have seen dozens of different plan formats that can be effective IF the people writing them will take the time to include quality content.

The formal planning process, whether in the form of a strategic plan, a marketing plan, a sales plan, or any other type of plan, provides the individual with the time and the environment to think about what has to be done in the future, thus avoiding the "ready, fire, aim" approach to business.

10) Business plans must be dynamic for both new and existing organizations. Almost everyone knows the importance of having a business plan when starting a new business. Further, most new businesses do develop some type of business or financial plan, often just to obtain financing or for recruitment purposes. Frequently these plans are very superficial and do not cover some of the key issues that need to be addressed. However, the issue is that, more often than not, a business plan becomes a document that is placed on a shelf (or worse, in a drawer) and never looked at once it has been written. This is a major mistake as the nature of a business, and more importantly, the environment in which the business is operating can change from year to year. Therefore, the discipline of reviewing the strategic direction of your business plan at least annually to see if there is a benefit to making changes is a necessary part of effective business management.

On a more tactical level, a good business plan should have a three-year revenue and expense forecast, often referred to as a Pro-forma P&L, which projects into the future rather than reflects what has happened in the past. Clearly, this revenue and profit forecast MUST be updated each year as part of the overall dynamic nature of the business plan exercise. Also, when considering the coming year(s) relative to the sales and marketing area, it is absolutely essential to take stock of what the company is doing in the third or fourth quarter of the current year and develop the specific programs that should be implemented in the coming year(s). This way, the plan can be well-thought-out in advance of implementation.

11) The larger span of control a manager has, the less effective the individual will be in managing the personnel for which they are responsible. The definition of management is to provide direction to people for whom the person is responsible and to help them to succeed in their position for the ultimate benefit of the organization. The number of individuals that one manager can supervise depends largely on the difficulty of the job they are supervising and the resultant amount of help they might need to be effective.

There is a generally accepted rule of thumb that for upper-level, white-collar type employment, a supervisor can effectively manage 3-5 people. This span of control can change dramatically based on the experience level of the subordinates and the degree of learning they will need to become effective. While the computer age enables managers to stay abreast with the performance of many more people than in the past, an effective manager will self-determine their optimal span of control based on the needs of the organization in terms of managing, training, and motivating the employees under his or her control.

12) It is almost impossible for a service organization to hire a "rainmaker" to increase the revenues of the business. It is very common to work with clients who really do not enjoy sales or do not feel they are very good at it, so they spend considerable time and money seeking to find someone who can do the selling so the owners can just work on projects. The fallacy in this thinking is that in virtually all situations, if an individual was an effective rainmaker (i.e., business generator), he or she would be in business for himself/herself rather than doing it for another organization. While I have experienced many situations where "prospective" rainmakers have been hired based on what they say on paper or in an interview (they have a great track record of sales and a strong prospect base), I have never seen this type of situation work out in the end for either the company or the individual.

13) Email communications tend to lend themselves to sloppy thinking and less than optimal recommendations. This is not to suggest that email is not a valuable part of the business process, but rather that the rapid response nature/expectations of this type of communication often do not result in providing the best quality thinking. You might even ask yourself how many times you wish you did not hit the SEND button, wishing you had spent more time on the communication before you sent it. Email is a great tool for quick responses to a simple question or to set up a meeting, provide directions, or ask a question to another person. However, I am a very strong believer that any communication to another individual that is really important or is complicated should be written in a word processing program and then attached to a cover email.

The discipline of having to create a document in a more formal, word-type format encourages the writer to think about the content more carefully, so it represents the best possible thinking. Another sign of the sloppy thinking associated with emails is the significant number of typos and poor grammar they contain, as people do not tend to proofread emails with the same attention to detail as they do a more formal document.

14) The strategic focus of an organization will be much more effective if those responsible for developing operational strategies commit them to paper in a formal document. It is so common to find that two or more people in the same company have a different idea about key strategic topics such as the definition of the target audience, the most important goal for the organization, the principal copy point that should be delivered in external communications or advertising. The reason for this is that almost always, the organization has not committed its strategies to writing and circulated them to the people who should be conversant in them. By committing the strategies to writing, it is the most effective way to obtain inputs from others in the organization and to ensure that the appropriate people are in agreement with and fully understand the direction identified in the strategy.

15) **Personnel in any organization will spend a disproportionate amount of time on those areas of their responsibility for which they are measured by their managers.** As a result of this, it is very important for a manager to understand that subordinates will normally give "lip service" to projects or areas of their responsibility which they do not feel are particularly important to their supervisors or will impact on their performance review/salary at the time of assessment. An example might be the assignment of a committee role at the corporate level (i.e., developing an employee handbook) where their supervisor is not involved and therefore gets little input as to the level of performance of their subordinates in the group. It is the responsibility of a supervisor to ensure that their subordinates operate in the best interests of the organization by completing all projects and responsibilities that are assigned... even if there is no direct relationship between the performance and the salary and bonus, which might be associated with it. This is one reason why the implementation of project lists is such a key tool for both managers and their employees.

16) **Senior management of an organization should think *defensively* with regard to the staffing of the institution.** This refers to the need to protect the organization from the loss of key personnel due to termination, promotion, or employee-initiated departure. An effective manager will protect

the company from a staffing problem via good management of the people he/she supervises (relative to titles, job descriptions, raises, bonuses, etc.), cross-training of subordinates to be qualified to cover more than their immediate areas of responsibility, and the identification of potential replacement personnel who can fill the shoes of the key personnel. This is referred to as *succession planning*. However, most organizations only consider this for the most senior people in the institution. In some organizations, the loss of a senior clerk could create many more problems in the short term than the loss of a Vice President.

17) **Good management skills are very transferable and generally are much more important than technical knowledge in a particular type of business when considering personnel for employment.** Every experienced consultant understands that there are basic principles of good management, and they are much more difficult to learn than the functional knowledge of a specific product category or business space. A smart individual can generally learn enough about a particular business in a relatively short time; however, it's is very difficult to teach someone how to be an effective manager if they do not already have these skills. An example of this from my consulting career might demonstrate this most clearly. In my almost fifty years in the consulting business, the most common question I would get at a new business meeting is what my experience is in the particular business for which I am trying to sign a new contract. You almost always hear the prospect tell you how important prior experience in the category is as they say, "our business is different from others for whom you have worked." I can say with complete confidence that after having worked with over 1000 different entities over the past 45+ years that there are basic principles of management that apply to all organizations regardless of the business in which they operate. An individual who has demonstrated strong management skills in the past in another organization or product category will almost always be able to learn a new business in a very short period of time by asking the right questions of the key people who can provide the best answers.

18) **It is essential for small businesses to have a strong #2 individual in the organization who is fully capable of taking over management of the company in the event the existing leader is not available.** Most small, and a large number of medium-sized companies, operate with a leader (Founder, President, CEO, etc.) and a staff of middle or lower-level personnel to run the company. While this can work very effectively in normal times, the situation would change very significantly in the event of the incapacitation of the leader. Perhaps the organization could function for a short time without the leader, but it is highly unlikely that this would be viable in the medium to long term. While some may view having a strong #2 leader/manager as an unnecessary expense since the company could continue to operate for some time without the leader, there is another very good reason why a strong #2 is an essential ingredient for a successful small company. In most cases, the real money from starting and running a small business comes when it is sold to a larger organization for a high multiple of earnings. The likelihood of successfully selling a company without a strong #2 leader/manager is very low, as an acquiring company will often want the current owner to leave in order to facilitate the assimilation of the acquired company. Therefore, the existence of a strong #2 becomes particularly important as the acquirer seeks to operate the new company. Further, the acquisition of a company that totally depends on the leadership of one individual is very risky, as the death or incapacitation of that individual would make the value of the acquired company significantly lower... particularly in the short term until a new leader has emerged.

19) **A small company should always be seeking potential acquisitions, as it is the fastest route for growth.** Traditionally, smaller companies tend to think of themselves as the target of acquisition activity rather than the one who is seeking acquisitions. However, there is no faster route to growth than by acquiring the right company as you can benefit from their revenue, profits, and potentially their personnel without having to absorb many of the overhead costs they have had to incur as a regular part of their operations. The management of smaller companies generally does not tend to think about acquisitions as they often do not have "extra" funds to spend to buy another institution. However, with creative financing (i.e., earn-outs, stock swaps, etc.), it is definitely possible for successful small companies to acquire others with relatively little cash on hand.

20) **There are some definite lessons I have learned about the process of terminating employees.** Specifically, it is important for management to maintain a detailed written record of the reasons why the employee is being terminated. Importantly, when a potential firing is anticipated, there should be an official file that identifies the performance or behavioral issues and the dates these have been identified. This record should be reviewed by an employment attorney or the company Human Resources department BEFORE the action is taken. One of the first thoughts of many (if not most) discharged employees is to sue the company to get additional money following termination. By having a comprehensive file on the employee, you can often avoid any attempted legal action, but if it does occur, you will have the facts on your side to justify the legal and fair termination.

Secondly, the employee should have a detailed exit interview with a senior member of the organization to explain why he or she is being terminated and to outline any severance package that would be offered. A thorough exit interview should be conducted not only with terminated employees but also with others that choose to leave based on personal reasons. Exit interviews can identify problems in the organization with regard to personnel, supervision techniques or processes, or procedures. With this information, management is in a position to correct problems that have been identified.

Thirdly, I have always been a believer that once you terminate an employee, they should leave the premises/organization that day. If they are allowed to stay, there is almost no good that will come of that in terms of the ill-will that they are likely to spread to others which whom they have been working.

21) **While remote working (i.e., from home) is the choice of many, if not most employees, it is very important to understand the major flaws associated with it.** The proponents of working from home say that the company gets more time from the workers as the time of the commute is eliminated. While this may be true in some very limited situations, my experience is that most people actually spend less time at their desks at home than they would in an office. This is because of the distractions of home (family, television, refrigerator, home gym, etc.) and the ease of not working since nobody would know. In addition, there are some other very strong negatives associated with working at home, such as:

- The loss of a corporate spirit de corps that comes when working in a group

- The increased difficulty of supervising an employee who is not in the same work environment

- The problems with trying to train a new employee when you are not in the same place

- The reduced likelihood of asking peers or supervisors their opinion on ideas that you have committed to them in writing in an official document

- The difficulty that a large percentage of people have with self-motivating and how that becomes magnified when working alone

- The loneliness that lots of people have when they are working alone, which can have a major impact on both morale and the quality of the work product

Marketing Research Lessons

1) **Marketing research should be viewed as a type of insurance, in much the same way that one looks at life insurance or property and casualty coverage.** The use of market research is essentially a tool available to help managers make better decisions. Theoretically, the more research conducted, the better the ultimate decision will be. Large, well-funded organizations spend millions of dollars on different types of market research each year to help them get the "right" answer. Smaller, less well-funded organizations tend to avoid most primary research (i.e., proprietary work done specifically for them), relying on published data from the government or trade associations and their own judgment. It has been my experience that many smaller companies would have been much better off if they could grasp the concept that market research is an *investment* and is a form of insurance that can avoid major expensive mistakes.

2) **The "ugly baby story" is one that everyone involved in marketing research should be cognizant of all the time.** This story addresses whether you ever have gone to visit a person who has just had a new baby and told the parents that they have an ugly baby. Clearly, nobody would ever do it. This relates to the field of marketing research from the perspective of the dangers associated with asking friends or relatives how they feel about a new product idea, a marketing concept, or a marketing program. It is virtually impossible to obtain a completely objective/honest answer from someone who knows you have a stake in the answer. This is just one reason why people should never do their own focus groups or in-depth interviews for a program, product, or concept in which you

have any financial or personal interest. The participants in the study will learn very quickly that you are not totally objective with regard to the inputs they provide.

3) **Anyone who is involved in using the internet to market a product or service must be intimately familiar with Google Analytics and specifically the metrics that are most important.** Most people who subscribe to Google Analytics (clearly the best of the internet analytical tools) focus mostly on metrics such as the users/visitors to a website, the bounce rate reported (% of visitors that only view one page), or the number of pages viewed. Some more sophisticated users look at other available metrics such as average time spent on a site, most common entrance and exit pages, etc. However, it is very rare that people will consider what I believe to be by far the most important metric that is available within Google Analytics. Specifically, this refers to the measure of "engagement." Engagement is the percentage of website sessions that are less than 10 seconds long. The premise is that an individual who is on a website less than ten seconds either got there by mistake or quickly left because they could not see the value of this site in light of their objectives. In essence, a "less than ten-second visitor" is not a visitor at all. According to a Google study conducted in 2020, approximately 62% of all visitors to websites remain on the site less than ten seconds. I have seen many instances when this number was as high as 85% or 90%. Understanding this metric puts on a whole new perspective relative to assessing the viability of a website. For example, if you find that 75% of your visitors stay less than 10 seconds, you should recognize that there is significant work to be done to get them to stay longer. For some reason, this "engagement" metric is almost never considered when people look at Google Analytics data. This is probably because it is not on the Google Analytics dashboard and requires some dig-

ging to find. In most cases (for some reason I don't understand, not all), this data can be obtained by going to Audience-Behavior-Engagement, where there will be a chart that shows the length of time on the site in roughly ten-second increments.

4) **When utilizing focus group research, the most important factor to consider is the quality and experience of the moderator.** Focus groups have become such a frequently used research technique in the current marketing environment that most organizations spend considerable time worrying about the number of groups to do and where the sessions should be conducted. However, for focus group research to be an effective technique, it must be managed and conducted by a highly trained moderator. Ideally, this is an individual who can not only facilitate a session but can develop a very thorough, comprehensive discussion guide and be able to provide action-oriented conclusions and recommendations after the sessions are completed.

Moderating focus is a *learned* skill that requires formal training both in technique and in listening skills. In today's environment, there are many people promoting themselves as focus group moderators but do not have the background and experience to provide added value to the research relative to the objectives for which it has been developed. The ideal background for a focus group moderator is an individual who has real-world marketing experience on the client side, and has been observed by experienced moderators who can impart the techniques for conducting successful groups. To this end, it is important to understand that a well-run focus group is NOT just a series of questions the moderator asks of the participants, but rather a discussion led by the moderator that generates interactions among the participants to delve into the "reasons why" behind the decisions they make as it relates to the subject of the group.

5) **It is essential that the person who conducts the focus group also commits to writing the report.** In the current marketing environment, it is very unusual for a moderator to write his/her own report. Most moderators provide audio or video tapes to others who write the actual report that the moderator provides to the client. After having personally conducted over 3000 focus groups, I can say without any hesitation that a focus group report written by the moderator should be dramatically better than one developed by a writer working from tapes. A skilled moderator is able to learn a great deal by being in the room and interpreting non-verbal communications by and among the participants.

6) **When planning a marketing research project, special attention should be placed on the composition of the participants.** If the right people are not included in the research study, the results will not be reliable. To this end, it is very easy to compromise on the specifications of participants due to the difficulty of finding some people, but poorly executed research is much riskier than no research at all. Focus group sessions work best with homogeneous participants who have been prescreened based on having common characteristics relative to product purchase behavior, demographics, and in some cases, the sex of the participants. To this latter point, there are some groups that should be single-sex sessions with individuals very close in age.

7) **Be very aware of the concept of "first-position-bias" when conducting market research studies.** First position bias is a known research issue in which the first stimuli presented to a participant in a research study will

almost always be preferred vs. the others that are present-ed. Therefore, if you are doing research among different concepts, packages, advertisements, etc., it is essential that the ideas presented be rotated or the results will not be correct. One specific example I encountered during my career was a packaging test for a soft drink I was involved in several years ago. The package designer favored one package and volunteered to submit it to customer re-search vs. another design option. Unbeknownst to me (I was the marketing consultant for the client), the package designer exposed their design first in all the research in-terviews that were conducted. As predicted, their design was the most preferred option. Two years later, another test was conducted for a diet version of the product, where the only change was the addition of the word "diet" adja-cent to the name. When the research was conducted on the diet version, the alternate design used before was the other option in the study. This research was conducted using item rotation as it should be, and the final results from the study were exactly the opposite of the original study. This will happen any time the discipline of employ-ing first position bias is used.

8) **When conducting taste test research, the protocol of the "odd cup" discipline must be employed if you are to obtain reliable data from the research.** Most product testing is conducted measuring reactions to product A vs. product B. This approach has great flaws, as you never know if the participants were even able to taste the differ-ence between A and B before they answered the questions. That is why it is much more prudent to use the "odd cup" approach. This methodology involves product taste testing that evaluates three items. Two of the three are the same, so the first phase of the research involves determining whether the participant can tell the difference between the items, product "A" and product "B." The sample is then divided in-

to two cells; one among people who could discriminate between the two products (i.e., identified the "odd cup"), and the other cell was among non-discriminators. In the second phase, where the goal is to identify which product (A or B) was preferred, experienced market researchers will use the data from the discriminator group as a more reliable indicator of real preference, as due to the odd cup process, they demonstrated a more educated palate than the other group.

9) **It is essential to obtain an advanced "buy-in" to research that is conducted to help with decision-making.** Some managers utilize research primarily to have information that will help to confirm their going-in bias. If the research does not agree with what they wanted it to say, it is common to blame the research (i.e., a bad sample, a bad focus group moderator, a poor questionnaire, etc.) rather than recognize that their initial view of the problem being evaluated was not correct. One real-world example of this was research (focus groups) that I conducted for a talk radio station in a major U.S. city. The station manager was interested in replacing the people who handled the 4 p.m.-7 p.m. time period (drive time), so we conducted research to evaluate an alternate approach to the current way the programming was implemented during this period.

The research clearly showed that the proposed new format was weak and did not appeal to the target audience. This finding was consistent in all groups that were conducted. However, the general manager of the station had convinced himself that the new format was a big improvement... even before the research was conducted. After getting the results, he discounted all the findings and decided to change to the new format, despite its poor performance in the research. The final result was that after the first contract (13 weeks), the new format was eliminated due to very poor performance, and the old programming was re-turned to the time period. The lesson here was that it would have been preferable to encourage the general manager to have an open mind going into the research and that he would accept the output of the research, even if it did not agree with his going-in feelings.

10) When conducting market research, it is essential to understand that the quality and value of participant responses are directly related to how close the "item" being evaluated is to the actual production quality product. This lesson has come back to me in the real world several times over the past 30-40 years. For example, if you are conducting research relative to advertising concepts, seeking to obtain reactions to the impact of an ad and trying to determine how effectively it communicates the key messages that were intended, this type of research can be conducted in many different ways representing varying stages of commercial development. Perhaps the most basic would consist of a drawing or a photo that illustrates the essence of the ad (print, radio, outdoor, etc.) accompanied by some copy that tries to communicate the key message. In this situation, the respondent is really given very little stimuli with which to respond, and while you might get some useful information from this very rudimentary research, it clearly will not be as good as it might be if the research were conducted with a more formal demonstration of the campaign. This could come in the form of a storyboard (pictures of different frames from the advertisement with words attached to each), a rough sketch of a print ad, or even an "animatic" (basically a storyboard put in motion) for a television commercial. The basic reason for this is that respondents do much better in comprehending what the real stimuli are when it is presented in a finished form. Another example of this same principle involves new product testing. There is some excellent information that

can be gained from exposing a rough drawing of the new product concept with a brief statement that describes what the product is and what benefit it offers, BUT if you can develop a working prototype of the product, the quality of the information will be dramatically better. As a general rule, the more well-developed the stimuli, the more reliable will be the responses from the research.

11) **There are some questions for which the reliability of the responses from participants must be viewed very carefully as they are extremely difficult to obtain accurately.** The two most common areas are efforts to determine *intent to purchase* and *to identify the optimal price* of a product or service. In both situations, there is research that can be used to provide some directional information (i.e., should it sell for $5.00 or $15.00; what percentage of people will actually buy the product), but in both cases, the only way to get very reliable information is to obtain it from a test market. Until a consumer has to pay for a product or service with their own money, you really cannot get a very accurate measurement of how many will buy and what the optimal price should be.

12) **It is also important to recognize that there are potential marketing research situations where the best decision is NOT to do any research.** One example would be a situation where the cost of the research would be so prohibitive that the results could be obtained more accurately, quicker, and cheaper by just going into a test market. Another example is when it is clear that the decision-makers requesting the research would not be objective relative to the results, as they had already made up their minds.

13) **I have always been a very strong opponent of online focus groups.** This is an alternative to in-person focus groups that have been utilized by some researchers for

several years. During the Covid period, there was no other viable option for in-person focus groups, and with the popularity of video platforms like Zoom, many researchers believe that the online option is an acceptable alternative to an in-person group. Those who feel that way do not really have a good understanding of how focus groups should be conducted and why anything other than the live in-person session is a very bad option. There are three key reasons why the live group is the ONLY way to conduct focus groups.

- First, in focus group research, the moderator is "king" and must be in total control of the session. It is virtually impossible to duplicate the role of the live moderator in a video session.

- Second, an experienced moderator will pick up on non-verbal clues in a live group that could never be obtained in the video version.

- Third, a well-conducted focus group happens when the bulk of the discussion is between participants and not simply a question-and-answer session from the moderator to the people in the group. The video format does not lend itself to ongoing interactions among the participants.

Sales Lessons

1) **Everyone in business, regardless of their position, is a salesperson.** Other than the individuals hired into an organization as "salespeople," it is very rare to encounter people in a company who recognize that they must develop excellent selling skills if they are to be effective in their job. For example, if you work in a factory on an assembly line, you will be more likely to be promoted to more responsible positions when you can demonstrate to your supervisor how valuable your contribution is to the organization. In effect, you are *selling* yourself. If you are the Chief Information Officer of a company and your responsibility is to manage the data processing in your company, you are still a salesperson. You need to have the skills to sell ideas, proposals, or personnel changes under your control. In almost every position in an organization, it is essential that everyone understand the importance of learning (and utilizing) selling skills so their effectiveness in the company can be maximized.

2) **It is vital that everyone in senior management and executive sales positions understand the difference between sales *training* and sales *education*.** Most sales organizations believe they are conducting sales training when they are actually implementing sales education. Sales training is a process whereby a senior sales executive would work with a field (or in-house) salesperson during the sales process. Specifically, the optimal type of sales training is when a sales executive demonstrates the optimal sales approach to the subordinate by actually conducting the sales interview while the salesman is observing. After the sales call, the "trainer" would sit down with

the salesman to discuss the process employed in order to establish the standards for a good sales call. The next step in the training process is for the salesman to conduct the next selling opportunity with the "trainer" along with observing the sales call. After this sales call (and as many more that are needed), the trainer and the salesman will take the time to discuss the elements of the call so the best practices are followed. This is the essence of *sales training.*

Sales *education* (which most organizations call sales training) is conducted when salesmen are provided with individual and/or classroom-type presentations, collateral materials, and other sales tools that are designed to educate the salesperson about product knowledge or sales techniques. The difference between this and sales *training* is the absence of an actual selling situation where the trainer demonstrates the right way to sell and tries to pass along the best techniques that the salesman should use. Both sales training and sales education are essential to developing a quality sales organization, but the more emphasis put on *training,* the better as it will be the element that will develop selling skills.

3)   **Price is almost never the real reason for losing a sale.** Anyone who has spent time interacting with salespeople will recognize that the most common reason that a sale was not made is that the *price was too high.* This is the easiest and quickest way to turn away a salesman. However, a detailed post-analysis of the sales situation probably would identify other reasons that the sales effort was not successful. The most common is that the salesman did not effectively communicate the *value* of the item (or service) they were selling. Specifically, did the salesperson identify the BENEFITS to the customer as virtually all purchase decisions are ultimately made based on "what is

in it for me"... the BENEFIT. Salesmen should be trained to understand that a "no" or a "price too high" reaction should be viewed as a request for more information and an indication that the salesperson is not doing an effective job selling value and BENEFITS, which could be very effective in helping to close the sale.

4) **One important lesson I have learned relates to all organizations where a buyer and a seller have face-to-face interactions. This involves the use of name tags by the selling (or servicing) individual.** The existence of a name tag changes the entire nature of the relationship between the buyer (or servicer) and the seller. One example would be a restaurant, in which case the server has a name tag. If you know the name of the person who is serving you, it is much easier to interact with that individual than if they are just a "miss" or a "sir." Another example might be a retail store where the person behind the counter has a name tag. You will have a much more positive interaction (hopefully ending up in a sale) if you address this person by name. This is a very simple idea, but one that can make a huge difference in the overall success of an organization.

5) **Sales incentive programs can be extremely effective in motivating salespeople to work harder to generate incremental revenues.** However, the key to successful sales incentive programs is to ensure that you only measure salesmen on metrics over which they have total control. For example, it is common for organizations to include a regional or national component in a sales incentive program with the thought that the group effort will be better if some compensation was based on how the others perform. It has been my experience that this type of program will not work. It is actually a disincentive, as an individual salesperson cannot control the performance of others, so

many would object to this program as they would feel that they are being penalized for the less-than-optimal performance of their peers.

An incentive plan payout must be able to be easily calculated in advance by the salesperson, so they know what to expect based on their performance. Therefore, using revenues, new account openings, or perhaps even calls made are something the salesperson controls and can measure against the plan objectives. Another major mistake that some organizations make is to focus sales incentives for salespeople based on the profitability they generate. Unless profitability is measured based on a sales-controlled metric such as average margin, there is no way a salesperson can have enough control over corporate profitability, thus making it a bad incentive measurement. Salesmen will work toward objectives for which they have control and will get rewarded for their performance. Any other scheme will not work to motivate salespeople to generate incremental sales.

6) **Sales incentive programs should be relatively short in duration, so the payout/reward/incentive provides an immediate motivation for incremental sales.** Incentive programs that are based on a month or a quarter are much more effective than those which last 6-12 months due to the impact of the frequency of reward in shorter plans. Further, the shorter plans are much easier for the salespeople to focus on, so they tend to have a much stronger impact on performance. Further, in the event a salesperson is having a bad week or month, they probably will not receive any money on the current incentive program, but they realize that their year is not ruined—they can catch up in a subsequent program.

One caution that needs to be considered is the possible attempt by some salespeople to hold sales from one period in order to put it in another time frame due to the presence of an incentive plan. This must be watched very closely by sales management to minimize the impact of this type of maneuvering. One way to avoid this is to announce the contest only a couple of days before it begins, so there is little opportunity to try to "play the system" in order to win.

7) **An effective sales manager will pay close attention to all the available statistics associated with salesmen for whom he/she has responsibility.** Specifically, when assessing a salesperson's performance, so many sales managers spend most of their time focusing on the revenues generated or perhaps the average margins from the sales. However, there are some other very important metrics that should be carefully evaluated by sales managers in order to really understand the salesmen's performance. Examples of these are the number of calls made (per day or week), the close rate of the calls (i.e., what percent were successful), the longevity of the relationship of the salesperson with the customer. The goal of all this analysis is to fully understand why the salesman has or has not been effective, so appropriate remedial action can be taken to fix the situation.

8) **When hiring new salespeople, it is important to focus more on the selling experience/track record of the individual than their experience in a particular type of business.** It is much easier to educate an individual about a product or type of business than it is to turn someone into an effective salesperson. While effective training can dramatically improve the effectiveness of a salesperson, there are some personal characteristics that are virtually impossible to teach someone. This includes such characteristics as the drive for success, the work ethic, the ability to stay well organized, the desire to please the supervisor, etc. Perhaps the most important of all characteristics

of an effective salesperson is the individual's attitude toward the sales process, in terms of being a self-motivated person who does not need supervision in order to succeed.

9) **Effective sales planning is an extremely important part of the selling process, yet I have found that it is rarely emphasized by sales managers.** This refers to the thinking and planning well ahead of a sales call to determine how the call is to be handled in terms of what product(s) will be discussed, what programs will be presented, and what the best logistics are to calling on customers when the selling is conducted on a face-to-face basis. The more planning that goes into a sales call, the greater the likelihood of success. This process of advanced planning is one key area where an effective sales manager can have a major impact on the salesperson IF the manager plans a surprise visit to the salesperson in the morning as the salesperson leaves his/her residence (or arrives at his/her sales desk) and reviews the plans that the salesperson hopefully had developed before the start of the selling day.

10) **When hiring a sales manager, it is essential that at least 50% of the job description involves "in the field" sales *training* with the salespeople.** Most sales managers with whom I have worked over the past 40+ years understand their role relative to sales *education* and tracking of sales performance numbers, but only a small percentage of them know how to properly *train* their staff and therefore do not consider this an important job responsibility. Many sales managers feel they are fulfilling their role just by accompanying a salesperson on a call, but they do not put the type of effort into traditional sales *training* as discussed previously.

11) **All sales forecasts for the next year should be developed based on a "zero-based" approach, rather than**

simply applying a percentage increase to the prior year and assuming this represents a reasonable approach to forecasting. Zero-based sales forecasting involves planning the next year based on the levels of business that are projected/anticipated from each of the existing accounts and then determining a reasonable number of new customers that need to be obtained in order to achieve the desired growth. Generally, a revenue forecast for an organization is based on senior management's direction as to the growth that is anticipated, and then it becomes the task of the line workers to determine how they are going to achieve the objectives desired. This is why the "zero-based" approach is valuable. As an individual brand or sales forecasts are developed, the most important factor is the amount of new business that must be generated and the assessment of line management as to whether this is a realistic expectation.

12) **Sales quotas are an essential part of the sales management process and should be employed with all salespeople who can impact on the amount of sales they generate.** There are some "sales" positions that are really just order takers, and there is no opportunity for selling incremental products/services. For this type of "salesperson," quotas would be virtually meaningless. However, for the bulk of selling organizations, the establishment of a sales quota for each salesperson should be an integral part of an organization's annual business plan. If management is following the "zero-based planning" approach, the anticipated corporate revenues for the business plan year should be based on the sales revenue projections of each salesperson. Sales quotas should be set with the objective of increasing the prior year's performance but should not be set so high that the individual feels they are unattainable, and therefore the quota can become demotivating.

Finance Lessons

1) **Receivables do not buy groceries!** The management of receivables is an area that is commonly mismanaged by a large percentage of client organizations with whom I have worked over the years. It is more common among smaller organizations but is definitely not limited to small companies. Receivables are the source of cash, and CASH IS KING in business. If you don't have sufficient cash to pay your bills, it does not matter how large the receivables are. A sale is not completed until the money is collected from the sale.

One example that highlights the importance of this was a client who had a very successful and aggressive sales organization with revenues increasing at impressive percentages each month. However, their problem was that they never had enough money in their account to pay themselves what they felt was a reasonable wage. Upon analyzing the business, I found that they did have an excellent sales track record, with most customers regularly placing orders, and the number of customers and size of the orders were continuing to grow. However, they were so busy with selling that they were not collecting. The value of their receivables was approximately 75% of their sales, and more than half of all receivables were more than 60 days old. They just did not place a priority on collecting the money from the sales. This was an easy fix, and the company quickly corrected its cash problem.

With regard to receivables management, I have always recommended clients prepare a monthly (or semi-monthly) aging report that shows how old receivables are for each of the accounts. For any receivables older than 60 days, I always recommend that clients do not do business with the account until they get current. In most situations where receivables get to the 90+ day level, it can be very difficult to ever collect this money. The key to remember is that receivables are like cash, except they are in someone else's pocket when they should be in yours.

2) **Small businesses should use a formal accounting program to keep track of sales revenues and expenses.** A large percentage of small businesses keep track of sales and revenues on a spreadsheet program like Excel or Numbers, which is very difficult to operate when trying to keep track of invoices, inventories, collections, etc. My recommendation is that all small businesses purchase an accounting program such as QuickBooks, as the program will easily help the client organization manage their business. It is very inexpensive when purchased as an online program and will be one of the best purchases your business ever made. Further, when tax time comes around, if the account has been properly utilized during the year, the process of preparing taxes or providing information to the accountant is dramatically less time-consuming and definitely more accurate than trying to run your business with paper-based records.

3) **A key lesson for both large and small companies is to consider outsourcing some of the functions in order to reduce overhead and often to improve the accuracy of activity.** While this is more likely to be applicable to small businesses, it also is very relevant to larger size companies as there are functions such as payroll, web development and management, and bookkeeping which are frequently better performed by outside specialist organizations.

Another area where outsourcing is often the best option is the advertising and media placement for a company, whether this relates to traditional vehicles (e.g., television, radio, outdoor and print) or digital advertising and marketing (e.g., Facebook, LinkedIn, Twitter, etc.). Human resources is another area that is often outsourced, particularly for small companies. Unless you are in a large company with an HR department, it is very difficult for senior management in a small to medium-size company to keep up with all the regulations regarding hiring and firing, in addition to the other government requirements needed to be addressed, such as same-sex bathrooms, minority hiring, sexual harassment, etc.

4) **Whether or not you have outsourced your finance function, it is essential that monthly statements are prepared for the business to provide senior management with the information needed to manage.** I have found that there are at least three financial documents that must be produced monthly (or bi-weekly) for management. They are:

    i.   An *Aging of Receivables Report* which will tell you about collections in terms of how much money you are owed that is 30, 60, 90, or 120+ days old. This will give direction to the responsible party to focus on debt collection as a vital part of the business.

    ii.   A *Profit and Loss Statement* with both monthly and year-to-date information. This is vital to see where the business is in terms of revenues generated and expenses by line item for the year to date. It will provide insights into what actions need to be taken to help the company become (more) profitable by year's end.

    iii.   A *Balance Sheet* which is essential to help you determine your cash situation and your liabilities (payables) for the year to date. It also will track your Aging of Receivables report relative to the trends in your collections.

In addition, some clients I have worked with maintain a pro-forma P&L document during the year, which will show the actual results as they occur and the projected revenues and expenses for the balance of the year. This is an excellent tool to evaluate how close you are to being on plan for the year or how much you might have to make up in order to achieve your yearly goals.

5)   **One of the most important lessons I have learned over the past 50 or so years working with and personally operating a small business is the importance of keeping overhead costs as low as possible.** In a small business particularly, Cash is King, and the lack of cash flow problems is one of the two most common reasons why new ventures do not succeed (the other is the lack of adequate knowledge about the business you are entering). This ties into one of the above lessons about outsourcing, but it also covers "nice to have" expense items like new furniture, excess customer/client entertaining, taking more office space than you need, or space that is just too expensive given the state of your venture. While it is always advisable to have office space for expansion, this should be accomplished very judiciously as it can easily be "the straw that broke the camel's back" for a new venture. A small (or new) business should try to operate "on a shoestring" in order to keep the cash requirements as low as possible until collections catch up with sales/receivables and there is an established positive sales trend that provides confidence to the management that profitable sales will continue into the future.

6)   **I always recommend that a small or start-up enterprise do business with a small, local bank rather than one of the large chain banks.** With a large chain bank such as Chase or Citi, your company will not be of sufficient importance to them (regardless of what they say), so you will

not get the best advice, the best service, or the best people handling your account. You will be much happier in a smaller bank where you will probably deal with more experienced personnel who may really care about developing a banking relationship with you.

A real-world example of this happened to me in January 2021 when I went to my local Chase branch to set up a d/b/a for my consulting business. I needed this so I would be able to cash checks made out to business as opposed to me personally. I had previously considered but rejected using other corporate forms such as an LLC or Sub "S" Corporation as I did not feel I needed the liability protection that these corporate forms provide. It was hard for me to believe, but the local Chase banker did not know how to set up this type of account and could not find someone in the main office to call to figure out what to do. I left and went to a smaller bank, First Republic, with whom I have dealt for years on other matters, and they were able to handle my situation in a very few minutes.

7) **A major lesson I learned from a financial "wizard" friend of mine related to the issue of bank service charges.** This lesson is probably more significant for larger organizations, and particularly for institutions that have multiple outlets (food stores, clothing stores, etc.), but it definitely is something that every company should understand. This friend operated a consulting business that only worked with organizations to help them reduce bank service charges. His entire income, which was substantial, was based on earning a percentage of the savings he would generate for companies just by helping them reduce bank service charges. Most companies pay very little attention to bank service charges, as they normally are not a large line item. However, over time they can add up and can reduce total profits. I have found that bank service charges are a

very negotiable part of the banking system and can be reduced, particularly if you do a significant amount of business with a particular bank. Banking is a very competitive business, and if bank service charges are questioned, it is very likely that they can be reduced, thus adding to the bottom line of the organization.

8) **One of the most frequent statements I have provided to both senior management and financial executives in client companies is to *know your numbers*.** This emphasizes the importance of senior management understanding every income and expense item on their profit and loss statement and balance sheet, and also being able to recall the key numbers of the business (i.e., revenues, profits, margins, etc.) from memory at any time. The "know your numbers" lesson is a result of working with clients who just have no clue what a specific line item (or two or three) means on their P&L. This is an indication that they do not spend enough time and attention to managing the business, and may be missing some key problems or opportunities. To this end, I strongly urge that all the senior management of an organization, whether large or small, have a daily dashboard that is easily accessed on their computer that summarizes the most important numbers in the business with which they should be familiar.

9) **There is a major financially related lesson that most organizations should have learned during the awful Covid crisis of 2020-2021.** This relates to business travel and the options that are available to an organization to save both time and money. During Covid, corporate executives (whether senior or lower level) did dramatically fewer business trips than pre-Covid. People learned that there were many meetings that could be implemented via video programs such as Zoom, FaceTime, or Google, and it could be almost as effective (but hugely less expensive and less

time-consuming) as a live meeting. The important lesson here is that travel should be viewed very carefully by all employees to ensure that the trip is really necessary and whether the same result could be accomplished using video conferencing.

10) **Another lesson I have learned is that many organizations keep much too much money in their working checking account because they are too lazy, too "busy," or too uninvolved in the details of the business to effectively manage corporate funds.** Clearly, it is easier to do nothing relative to managing cash, particularly during a period like the 2020s when there are not a lot of safe places to earn a reasonable interest on your money. However, in working with client companies, I have found that it is not unusual for an organization to maintain a 3-6 month cash requirement in a corporate checking account that is earning no interest income. While the rate of interest in safe investment vehicles is very low at the current time (2021), there are some options available for "excess" capital, which will earn some interest and still be liquid (i.e., CDs, T-Bills, etc.).

Social Media Lessons

1) **Social media is like a flu shot.** It is free to use, but you really cannot tell how effective it will be. This is why every organization should pay attention to the trends in social media and utilize products/platforms that have become a major part of the marketing programs for most of the major corporations in the world over the past 10-15 years. Social media marketing is one area that can easily be outsourced to service companies that can manage this effort for companies that do not have qualified internal resources with these skills.

2) **Social media is not a panacea! Nor is it the "magic bullet" that so many businesspeople feel will solve problems that they experience that were caused by the absence of an effective "traditional" marketing program.** Used appropriately, social media can be an important part of the marketing mix, but for it to work for a brand, company, or service organization, it must be used as *part* of a marketing program, not THE marketing program. Over the past ten or so years, I have encountered many small and medium-size business executives who believe that all they have to do is put a website on the Internet or open a Facebook page, and their company will be automatically programmed for success. It can be difficult to explain why their website does not immediately get thousands or millions of visitors, as they often fail to recognize there are more than 100 million websites in cyberspace. While social media of all types provides the *opportunity* to reach millions of people throughout the world, achieving a significant social media audience generally requires a significant amount of money to generate awareness of your site.

Further, any element of a social media program (i.e., websites, Facebook pages, Instagram, etc.) should be part of an overall marketing effort that integrates each of the vehicles, so they provide synergy to each other for the benefit of the brand or company.

3) **A major lesson I have learned over the years is that effective websites must SELL the idea, the product, or the service and that very fancy designs for websites can look pretty but often will not *sell*.** This lesson refers to both e-commerce and non-e-commerce websites. The emphasis of a website must be on the product/service and the message that you wish to communicate. If this is not very clear immediately, the website will probably never be an effective marketing tool. A website is one example of a marketing tool where the "product is hero" lesson discussed previously really is obvious. If a visitor cannot tell within 5-10 seconds what the product, service, or idea is that you are trying to communicate on your website, you need to redesign your site.

4) **A website must get the attention of the visitor *immediately,* as the vast majority of people who visit websites do not remain on the site for longer than 10 seconds.** According to an internal source from Google, a worldwide study was conducted in 2020, which indicated that 68% of all people who visit a website remain on the site for less than ten seconds. There is almost nothing one can communicate in under ten seconds when opening a website, and therefore, while the "less than 10-second visitor" is counted just as much as a 2-minute visitor, they are very different people. In my judgment, the most important data that is available from Google Analytics (the tool that measures website metrics) is the *engagement,* which is defined as the percentage of sessions that last longer than ten seconds. Most people never examine their

engagement numbers but consider website traffic (i.e., to-tal visitors) and *bounce rate* as the key metrics to be eval-uated. However, it is evident that the percentage of web-site sessions that are longer than ten seconds gives a much more accurate view of the consumers' behavior on your website than any other metric available in Google Analytics.

5) **The key to successful utilization of social media is def-initely the quality of content you provide.** This refers to websites, blogs, Facebook pages, LinkedIn, and any other written content that you distribute on the Internet. It is the quality of content you offer that will determine whether visitors return to your site, read your blogs or interact in any way with the written material you put into cyberspace

6) **One of the most important lessons I have learned from many years of involvement with the Internet is the importance of *testing* and the ease of doing this in the cyber world.** Whether you are using the Internet for e-commerce, to build awareness of your enterprise, or to drive visitors to a store, a website, or a telephone number, your efforts will be much more effective if you take ad-vantage of the ease of testing different messages and ap-proaches which are available. Importantly, the Internet enables organizations to inexpensively test many different variables and have the results from the test almost imme-diately. For example, if the goal of your effort is to generate clicks to a URL or calls to a telephone number using a platform such as Facebook (with Facebook ads), you can test different visuals, pricing, spending levels, and many other variables that will ultimately enable you to maximize the potential of your Internet marketing efforts.

7) **If your goal is to build equity in your e-commerce product, it is almost impossible to accomplish this**

without selling the item(s) on your OWN website. Equity is defined as the value to your brand name and image so that you are selling more than just product X—you are selling branded product X, which your consumers attribute value to because the brand is well known and has established a persona. As consumers, we face the equity situation every day, whether we are shopping in a retail clothing store, a hardware store, or a supermarket. For example, when you purchase bleach, you can buy the branded Clorox bleach or the private label brand, which will be less expensive. The Clorox bleach exists today because the company has built equity in the name Clorox which gives their bleach an implied value, even though bleach is bleach, and there is no difference in the branded vs. the private label. Once you have developed equity in the name of your product, service, or company, it has a value that can be sold separately and apart from the actual product or services in the company.

The development of equity is particularly important when considering an e-commerce business, as there are many options available for selling your product(s). For example, you could sell your brand name WIGIT on Amazon, eBay, or Etsy (just to name a few very popular platforms), or you could sell it on your own site. The advantage of selling through the platforms mentioned is that in the short to intermediate term, you have the opportunity to generate sales volume if you can break through the clutter and get noticed by the millions of visitors to those sites. If you are also selling on your own site at the same time, the volume you generate will probably be dramatically less in the short to intermediate term. This is because sites like Amazon, eBay, and Etsy already have extensive traffic and your site has to begin generating visitors.

The advantage of selling on the existing sites is the traffic they have and the volume you might generate in the very crowded, competitive environment they represent. However, while you might generate sales, you probably will not develop *equity* in your brand due to the environment in which it is sold. When products or services are sold from a proprietary website where everything carries your brand, the name will begin to develop equity over time, as buyers will come to your site because of the items you offer. Further, when they come to your site to buy, the profit margins for you are much higher than selling on the other sites (due to the commissions they receive from the sales), and importantly you have control over your customer in terms of the service they receive. You do NOT have control over customers buying on Amazon, Etsy, or most other community sales sites.

While it is difficult, time-consuming, and expensive to generate traffic on your own website, over time, this can be a much better way for you to sell. With a proprietary site, you have the opportunity to build imagery and character for your brand (i.e., equity), which is something you have the opportunity to see in the future for a multiple of your profits, thus justifying the effort to build the equity in the brand.

8) **One of the major lessons I have learned relative to the use of any Internet advertising platform (i.e., Facebook, Instagram, LinkedIn, etc.) is that every ad must have *three* very important characteristics if they are going to be successful.** The first characteristic and most important element of any ad on the Internet is to have a very strong "call to action." Unlike traditional print advertising, a viewer is unlikely to be exposed to a specific Facebook ad (for example) more than one time in a week or two. Therefore, it is essential that when your target customer is exposed to your ad, you provide a sufficiently strong motivation for them to make a purchase immediately, rather

than hoping they will write down the offer and complete the purchase at another time. A "call to action" is an offer that is so sufficiently strong that it motivates the visitor to ACT NOW. Examples of a call to action might be a significant percentage discount off the regular price, a dollar discount, a free item when you purchase one at the full retail price in the next 24 hours, etc. It is also important for the call to action to contain a relatively short term (i.e., two weeks, ten days, etc.) termination date for the offer, as that will help to motivate a viewer to act now before they lose out on the discount.

The second characteristic that an effective Internet ad MUST have is a very compelling image that communicates your product or service in a very arresting way. To use Facebook as an example, most people go through Facebook very quickly, and if your ad does not have *stopping power*, you will not get enough people to be exposed to what you are selling to be able to take advantage of the call to action discussed above.

The third characteristic that the ad MUST have is a short *headline idea* in bold type at the top, which will help to work with the image to generate interested viewers. An example of a headline idea might be: "New men's razor, guaranteed not to cut," or "Introducing the latest hearing aid technology for guaranteed better hearing."

9) **Another key lesson I have learned in recent years is the importance of using synergy to increase the overall effectiveness of your social media efforts.** For example, when you publish a blog, effective use of postings on Twitter can be very effective in increasing the readership of your blog while building traffic to your website. I have been advising clients for many years that a key to maximizing the effectiveness of your blogs is to develop a

tweet based on the headline idea from the blog and tweet about the blog several times during the first week or two after publication. Naturally, you will want to hashtag the key elements of the tweet so that the audience has the potential to be larger than just your followers. Also, you should take advantage of the URL truncators bit.ly or adf.ly to shorten your URL, thus giving you more characters to describe your headline idea. The goal would be to have the truncated URL return the viewer to the blog on your website, with the hope of migrating them to the key areas of your website after having been stimulated by the contents of the blog

10) **I have never believed that using Twitter as a vehicle for retweeting other people's work is in the best interest of your effort to build brand equity or generate awareness of your product or service.** While many people feel that they are helping their cause by retweeting something they find in the secondary information marketplace, I feel this does little for your brand/product or company, as readers focus on the material you retweeted rather than generate positive thoughts about you for sending out this message. You are MUCH better off tweeting your own material, so the content is associated with your company and can help to build awareness and equity in your brand name.

New Product Development Lessons

1) **Avoid the urge to introduce a new product or service until all aspects of the product/service AND the marketing program are as close to optimal as possible.** When developing a new product or service, there is generally a great deal of excitement built up, and with it, a strong urge to introduce the new entry as quickly as possible. As a result, organizations often make the mistake of introducing the new entry before it has been proven that the product is right, the marketing plan has been developed, and the sales and distribution issues have been worked out. This can kill a test market and possibly be the death blow to the entire new entry introduction. In most cases, it is better to wait additional weeks or even months to be sure that all elements of the marketing mix are optimal before exposing an "almost-right" program to the target customer. This is because the target customers will generally try it one time, and if it does not meet expectations, the cost and time to get them to try it again can be significant. Or, if the marketing effort has not been optimized, it is possible the new entry will not get the trial it needs to be successful.

In most cases, being first to market represents only a short-term advantage, particularly if it is necessary to make changes in the product or the marketing program early in the life of the product (or service). Often the second or third to the market ends up as the category leader as they can learn from the mistakes of the early introducers and improve on them. One excellent example of this is the introduction of the Blackberry smartphone. They were the first high-tech entry into this field, and at one time, the name Blackberry was synonymous with a personal assistant device. However, today, Blackberry has retreated into a very specialized area, and the iPhone has become the standard of the industry.

2) **Whenever possible, test your idea in a very small, controlled (test) market rather than assume you have it right and go national (or international) right away.** While there definitely is a natural concern that the competition will steal your idea and introduce it nationally before you finish your test/control introduction, in most cases, the risk of waiting is well worthwhile. Testing gives you the benefit of making changes in your product and/or marketing program before you go full out with the introduction, thus enabling you to have a much better chance of ultimate success. Further, by testing your new entry in a small area, the amount of money you put at risk is much less than if you were to go to market without first testing your program.

3) **A key new-products lesson I have learned is that the price of a product or service in the test should be the same price that it would have if the product or service were at full production.** This lesson applies as much to an e-commerce product sold on your or someone else's website as it would if the product is a new type of soup, toothpaste, computer, or scalable service business. When developing test market costs for an item, it is a given that the production cost of a small quantity will be much higher than it will be for a large quantity. However, it is essential to conduct the test based on the cost structure of the full production item, or you will never really know how the product/service will perform in an actual marketplace with the correct pricing. While this will almost always guarantee that you will lose money in the test market (due to the much higher product costs and lack of efficiencies

relative to elements of the marketing program), the loss should be anticipated and figured into the total economic model for the introduction.

An example of this would be a widget that you plan to produce in Asia due to the dramatically lower costs than you would be able to realize if your manufacturing were in the U.S. However, for the purpose of the test market, you probably would be much better off producing it in the U.S., recognizing that you will pay more per item than if it came from Asia. You would use the Asian manufacturing costs to figure out your test market pricing so you can test the same marketing plan that you would ultimately have if the test is successful. Another advantage of using the higher unit cost item produced in the U.S. is that you would be able to purchase much smaller quantities than you would for an item coming from Asia.

4)   **When moving from test market to full-out national or international marketing, it is advisable to conduct customer research among individuals who have had sufficient time to go through at least two to three purchase cycles.** With some products, such as appliances or vehicles, this is not possible, but for many new products, it is a very prudent step to take. The reason is that you do not want to read your market incorrectly, believing that the high sales generated in the early months represent a very satisfied customer base, and the new product is destined to be a huge success.

A real-world mini-case study that emphasizes this point was the introduction of Piels Beer in the 1950s. This was a lager beer that had been around for decades as a small-share item appealing to people with a very specific German beer taste. The company decided to dramatically increase exposure of the product in the mid-1950s and hired Young

& Rubicam to develop advertising as part of a major effort to the brand. The agency developed advertising using spokesmen named Bert and Harry Piels. The team was a well-known comedy pair (Bob & Ray) who were extremely popular, and the advertising campaign was amazingly successful. The program very quickly built the awareness of the Piels brand, and the sales shot up immediately and for the first few months. The company felt they really had succeeded with the introduction, and their beer would become popular again. Then after several months of this successful advertising and the resulting increase in sales, the bottom fell out of the program, and the sales dwindled to almost nothing. By about 1962, the brand was history.

A key problem was that the company did not do effective marketing research during the introductory period to understand the consumer dynamics of the brand. Apparently, the very effective advertising was the primary stimuli that killed the product well before its time, as the research that followed showed that most of the triers did not like the beer. The rising sales numbers were reflective of the trial that the great advertising generated, but the research found that the repeat purchase level was very low. Therefore, once the advertising had reached the target market of triers, there were no repeat purchases, and the brand's sales growth dropped precipitously.

5) **When developing new products, the most important consideration is whether there is a real, long-lasting consumer market for the item.** While it might seem very obvious to most people, there have been many new product failures that resulted from scientists and engineers developing what they felt was a superior product, but not utilizing target customer input to determine if the item had "legs" and could develop a franchise that would last many years. An interesting example of this was a mousetrap

that operated similarly to the standard wood and wire traps that have been around for over 100 years. However, this mouse trap was dramatically better in that it was easier to load, did not release without a mouse head inside, and was guaranteed to finish off the mouse when caught. Apparently, the developer of this trap learned that it was not unusual for the old-time traps to maim but not kill the mouse. Also, their many buyers disliked the traps because they sprung on the buyer's fingers while setting up for the mouse.

This superior mousetrap was a disaster for the company. The primary reason for the product failure was traced to the fact that the engineers developed a great product but did not spend sufficient time doing in-home research with consumers to test reactions to the invention. This "better" mousetrap was premium priced vs. the traditional trap, and it was intended to be used multiple times and had a built-in easy-release latch that enabled the homeowner to discard the dead mouse and reuse the trap. However, what the post-mortem research revealed was that homeowners had absolutely no interest in reusing the trap, as they would have to clean off the blood and other body fluids that occurred due to the impact of the immediate death of the mouse. As a result, research indicated they would rather discard the trap with the mouse rather than use it again. Thus, another case of a new product that probably would have made it to market had the pre-introduction research and planning been focused on the consumer reactions to the product prior to introduction.

6) **Percentage off or dollar discounts employed during the early part of a new product introduction are frequently of questionable value to the target customer.** This is because there is no existing or predetermined VALUE of the discount since the item is new to the market. This type

of promotion tends to be viewed as a price reduction rather than an incentive to try. For example, to offer $10 off the price of a regularly priced $40 item does not have nearly the same impact in the introductory period on the customer as it might at a later time when there is some sense of what the $40 product is really worth.

7) **A key lesson I have learned relative to new product introductions is that year one's marketing strategy should be focused on building awareness of the product or service, with a secondary goal of achieving trial.** The awareness-building effort should seek to deliver one (or at most two) copy points about the item, which will differentiate it from other similar products in the market. Once this is achieved via multiple exposures to the advertising, the focus of the marketing should be on generating the product trial. It is for this reason that when introducing a new product, it is generally much more advantageous to seek to obtain the purchase of ONE item, rather than develop a trial program that attempts to stimulate the purchase of multiples (i.e., $3.00 off on the purchase of three widgets). This is the reason that promotions such as free product samples, sample size items for purchase, and very low introductory pricing (aimed at eliminating any risk of trial) are essential parts of many new product introductory programs. To this end, after approximately 3-5 months of a product introduction, it is absolutely essential to conduct consumer research among the target audience to determine the level of awareness (aided and unaided) of the item and the extent to which the product trial has been obtained. Further, the attitudes of the triers are vital to the future, as their future intent to repurchase is the difference between success and failure

8) **Perhaps the most important exercise in the new product/service development process is the development of**

a rough proforma P&L early in the development phase. This is to ensure that a successful introduction will achieve the objectives of the introduction (i.e., normally to make money by building a market or taking share from others in the category). During my 11 years working with over a thousand different clients at SCORE, I encountered dozens of new product entrepreneurs who had very interesting new product or service ideas, but they never did the up-front exercise to determine if there was likely to be sufficient demand for the item to generate a meaningful business. Often the new business idea was very interesting and probably would be something very good for mankind, but we were able to figure out very quickly that there was no possible way to make money with this effort.

While the estimate of market potential for new product concepts is normally based on a series of assumptions (i.e., target market size, percentage trial in the first three years, repurchase rates, etc.), it is very beneficial to go through the exercise of projecting the possible market potential for the product or service before spending huge amounts of money on research and development to develop an item that is probably DOA (dead on arrival). An example I often use with clients is the individual who was interested in opening a typewriter repair shop. In 1950 this might have been a very good business, but in the current computer/word processing environment, an entry like this is DOA. While this is a very obvious situation, I have encountered well over 100 different new product or service concepts that were domed before they ever went to market because of the lack of demand, the difficulty/impossibility of finding buyers, the difficulty of manufacturing, or the absence of a viable price-value relationship.

9) **Entrepreneurs who develop new products should be more concerned about obtaining quality customer research**

about their idea than the risk that someone who is exposed to the product or service before the introduction (i.e., during the research phase) will steal the idea and take away their potential market. While it is possible someone could steal an idea from you, based on their participation in market research, in my 45+ years' experience, the likelihood of this happening is DRAMATICALLY less than the benefits the entrepreneur would get from the exploratory customer research prior to the introduction. Protection of a new product idea is greatly overemphasized by most inventors, and therefore they can get bogged down with difficult NDA's or restrict the use of customer research that will help them introduce the best product possible. To give some specific support for this, I have conducted well over 3000 focus groups in my career. On average, there are 8-9 people in a group, and about half the sessions I conducted were relative to new product assessments. This results in exposure of new product concepts to 13,500 people, assuming only one idea is presented in each group (which frequently is not the situation). However, I have never experienced a situation where a new product idea, which we discussed in a focus group, was stolen by one of the participants and introduced before my client was able to bring theirs to market.

10) **Craft fairs, street fairs, farmers' markets, and other similar venues can be an excellent way to test the viability of some new products without having to invest significant money to enter a test market.** Over the course of my consulting career, I have worked with many clients who had developed a new product that lent itself to testing in the informal environment of the venues identified previously. Given that the ultimate test of a new product is whether customers will buy your product if it can be put into a real marketplace where the success depends on whether the consumer will actually pay for it (as

opposed to expressing their views in an "intent to pur-chase" questionnaire) the results can be very useful.

One recent example involved an assignment with a very talented graphic designer, who believed that beautiful de-signs on yoga mat bags were a sure thing in the current yoga craze that exists in many large U.S. Cities. In the ear-ly stages of this project, we visited local yoga studios and talked with teachers and students about this idea. The re-sponse was always enthusiastic both toward the idea of the bag and also relative to the fabulous designs that were created on the bags. To test the consumer reaction to this idea in a "real world" environment, we entered a three-day gift/craft show held every year in the Lincoln Center Plaza (surrounded by all the buildings at Lincoln Center) in New York City. We felt this was an excellent testing venue as the show generated large crowds (50,000+) and was in a city that had a high incidence of yoga studios and partici-pants. Further, because it was held over three days, we would not get misleading information in the event that weather became a factor to spoil one of the days. A very attractive, stylish booth was constructed with many differ-ent designs, and the bags were priced based on prior re-search in the New York market. At the end of the three-day show, my client received glowing comments about her designs from many different people, but she sold only three bags. One did not have to be a new products expert or a rocket scientist to determine that this was very likely NOT a viable concept. We felt that over three days, we should have sold at least ten per day to demonstrate some meaningful level of real consumer interest. In our post-mortem, we had lots of good research information based on comments obtained over the three-day event, but we still only sold three bags despite the large amount of traffic to the booth, so my client closed the business.

11) **When considering the introduction of a new product/new service, the most important element of the introduction is whether it offers a clear BENEFIT to the target consumer.** Consumers of all types make decisions based on the benefits that products or services they purchase provide for them. A benefit should be viewed as "what is in it for me." Some examples might help crystallize this very important concept.

A new drill has been developed to be sold in hardware stores. The key communication for this product should be whether it will help the target customer make better holes. The benefit of a drill is the holes it makes. Perhaps this new drill is made of a special material that will give it a longer life. If so, then the message should focus on the benefit of great holes for a longer period of time, rather than the technology associated with the drill or the new material used to manufacture the drill.

Another example is a new product in the writing category, which is a fountain pen that is made with a new type of ink delivery so it will never leak. The communication about this new pen should focus on the consumer benefit (will never leak) rather than the technology involved in avoiding leaks. The technology is the "reason why" it does not leak, but the communications about this pen should focus on the pen not leaking (the consumer BENEFIT).

A new corporate accounting system has been developed for online delivery to small or medium-sized businesses. The key benefit of this accounting program is the simplicity of the software, thus enabling the target customer to quickly get operational with the program, so it will be easy to keep track of revenues and expenses and easily produce various reports for the business. The BENEFIT of this new system is the ease of learning the system in a product category where most people find it relatively difficult to really understand the available accounting programs. In summary, the customer benefit of this new accounting package is the ease of use (i.e., what's in it for me) rather than anything relating to what the developer did to make it easier to use.

12) **One of the most valuable tools in the new products planning and development process is the PERT or GHANT chart.** There are many fancy words that describe what this is, but the document is essentially a flow chart of all the activities that must be accomplished in the new product development process if the product or service in question is to effectively make it to market. The principle behind this chart is very simple, but developing an effective chart is quite difficult.

The chart has two axes with the "X" axis representing all the weeks from the present time until the week the new product is introduced. They should be listed across the top, with the Monday being the date meant to represent the week. The "y" axis represents a listing of everything that must be done for the introduction to make it happen. Once all the items are listed vertically on the "Y" axis, the challenge is to identify when everything needs to get done. For example, a name must be chosen for the product or service (which would be listed as name selection), and the brand identity/logo also has to be created. Clearly, you cannot start the brand identity until you have the name, so the chart will show the beginning and end of one activity that must happen before the other can begin. Below is an example of a small part of a PERT chart used in new product development.

Brand X Pert Chart

3/1, 3/8, 3/15, 3/22, 3/29,
4/5, 4/12, 4/19, etc. etc. etc.

Select name   xxxxxxxxxx

Name Research   xxxxxxxxxx

Develop Logo   xxxxxxxxxx

Test Logo with Target   xxxxxxxxxx

Develop Pro Forma P&L   xxxxxxxxxx

Etc., etc.

Consulting Lessons

1) **An experienced consultant should never be intimidated by the client's statement that "our business is different than anything you have ever experienced."** In the almost 50 years I have spent in the consulting business, I have found that the vast majority of new client assignments start with the primary client contact trying to emphasize how different their business is from any other in your client list, thus requiring you (the consultant) to recognize this fact before you begin the assignment. However, while almost every business has its own unique elements, the basics of managing a successful business do not vary much by the type of business. The principles of good business management are essentially the same whether you are a soft drink bottler, a jewelry manufacturer, a retail clothing store, or a medical practice. An experienced consultant should be able to ask the right questions and seek the most important type of information in a relatively short period of time, so it is possible to be an effective "business doctor" to the client company. While prior experience working in a particular business, either as a consultant or a line operating person, is helpful, the most important characteristic of the consultant you hire is that he/she has the experience and intelligence to quickly learn the information necessary to be an effective advisor.

2) **The most important characteristic of an effective consultant is the ability to listen.** Having supervised consultants for many years, I find one of the major mistakes that a consultant makes is to develop a solution to a problem before he/she really understands the complete situation that exists. This is because most consultants feel they

have a need to demonstrate to their client how smart or effective they are very quickly, and often this can create major issues as the client assignment proceeds. Had more time been focused on active listening before making a judgment, a consultant would be much better prepared to help clients. My advice to all consultants is to spend approximately the first 25% of a contract period asking questions and listening very carefully to the answers before developing a point of view relative to a solution that might solve the client's problem.

3) **A major lesson I have learned in the consulting business is to start at the lower levels of the client company and work your way to the top relative to information.** It is so common in the consulting business for the consultant to begin an assignment by spending many hours with senior management getting the "lay of the land." However, I have always advised consultants to operate exactly the opposite. For example, when trying to figure out why a package goods food company's sales were not growing, the consultant has the option of meeting with senior management to get their views or going into the field to talk to the field sales personnel to obtain their view of the dynamics of the situation. In my opinion, the field sales approach is definitely the best approach as you can develop a good sense of what the various sales personnel feel is hurting the program, and you also should be able to assess how effective the sales personnel are in their jobs. By spending this time in the field, you will be in a much better position to develop a comprehensive series of questions to ask of the senior management. Often, those in the head office are focused on the sales numbers but do not spend the time to really understand what is happening "where the rubber meets the road."

4) **A key lesson I have learned in my years in the consulting business is to never *negotiate your fees*.** It is essential that a consultant develop a fee structure that is reflective of their expertise and experience and to stick with this pricing even if it means losing some assignments. It is very common for a client to ask you if you can do the assignment (for which you developed the proposal) for "x"% less, as they claim funds are tight, their budget has been cut, or they have worked with less expensive consultants in the past. I have always maintained that the fees in my proposal are what is needed to achieve the goals of the assignment and that no "fat" is built into the project. Further, I often communicate that the fees are based on a very detailed analysis of the time involved to complete the assignment, rather than some arbitrary figure that was developed with virtually no research.

If it is necessary to reduce the cost of the assignment due to the budgetary limitations of the client, this should be accomplished by eliminating some of the elements of the engagement so the time involved is reduced, thus a lower cost. Another very important reason why it is an awful idea to negotiate fees is that once you do this, you have communicated to your client (or the marketplace) that you are willing to negotiate and will end up doing this with every proposal you ever write for this client... and perhaps others who might hear about your practice of negotiating fees.

5) **I feel very strongly that a consultant should neither pay nor accept referral fees from other consultants.** It has always been my policy never to deal with referral fees, as I feel they take away the professionalism that should be associated with the consulting business. I only refer other consultants when I feel they are the best alternative for the organization to whom I am referring them. Similarly, I

would hope that nobody would refer clients to me because of the expectation of a referral fee. I believe that when referral fees are employed, it takes away from the objectivity of the referral and does not give the referred party the sense that you have chosen the organization because they are the best answer to the needs of the client.

6) **Responsiveness to the needs of your clients is, in my judgment, one of the most important characteristics of a successful consultant.** Essentially, this refers to the value the consultant places in responding to the requests of clients in a VERY timely fashion. It is a key factor in building rapport with the client organization, and it communicates to the client that you really care about helping them. A committed consultant recognizes they are in a *service business,* and the more successful consultants will be available to clients at any time. I have always told my clients that they can get to me 24/7, and in almost 50 years, I have had only one client habitually take advantage of my time.

7) **A successful consultant/consulting practice will maintain a constant effort to develop new business, even if the present workload is extremely challenging and time-consuming.** Almost every consulting practice is a cyclical business with high points and low ones. A mistake that most consultants make is to dramatically reduce or eliminate new business development activities when they are busy with existing client assignments. The optimal situation would be for consultants to always keep their focus on the future, as all consulting assignments come to an end, and if you have not been prospecting while you are completing existing assignments, you could face a situation of having virtually no business when the present assignment(s) are completed.

8) **One of the biggest mistakes that consultants make is to write proposals without receiving some budgetary guidelines from the prospective client.** Due to the desire to continually have client assignments, some consultants jump at any opportunity to submit a proposal for a potential assignment. However, I have learned that the chances of writing a successful proposal are dramatically reduced if you do not have guidance as to the client's budgetary requirements. Further, writing a comprehensive proposal can be very time-consuming, and without a sense of a budget for the project, you can spend huge amounts of time writing proposals that never get accepted, OR even worse, are accepted but not at a pricing level that is acceptable to you. In almost every area of the consulting business, there are generally many different ways to fulfill the requirements of an assignment. The difference between a $25,000 assignment and a $50,000 might simply be the amount of primary or secondary research you do or the time you spend interviewing client personnel. They both can provide meaningful recommendations to the client organization, but the amount of detail and the confidence associated with the consultant's report will be much higher if there is an opportunity to have time to conduct more interviews, do more research, or develop more alternative scenarios to give the client options relative to next steps. Therefore, it is in the best interests of both the client and the consultant to establish budgetary guidelines before a proposal is developed. My approach to clients in this regard has always been: "I can do this assignment several different ways, and the approach I take will depend on the amount of time I need to complete the work. The time required is what generates the fee for the assignment, so if I am provided with a budget amount in advance, I can plan a project work plan and write a proposal that is consistent with the budgetary parameters of the client.

9) **One of the strongest tools a consultant has relative to building a practice is an excellent *elevator speech*.** The elevator speech is a 20-30 second articulation of what your business is and what BENEFITS your clients will get from hiring your company to do the work. The genesis of the elevator speech is that you walk into an elevator and meet a long-lost acquaintance who asks you what you are doing with your life... as the elevator door closes. The goal of the elevator speech is to be able to provide enough information to this individual before the elevator reaches the floor when they get out. As a consultant, there will be many times per day, week, or month when you meet someone who inquires about what you do for a living. The elevator speech should be a totally rehearsed but natural 20-30 seconds about your consulting business that you can communicate to another person what type of consulting services you provide, and most importantly, the BENEFITS they would get from hiring your company.

10) **An experienced, quality consultant will never provide their client with a "knee-jerk" reaction to a new idea without taking the time to evaluate it thoroughly.** It is very common for consultants to feel they must have an immediate answer, or at least a strong opinion, about a new idea presented by their client. However, the more seasoned consultant will take the time needed to thoroughly evaluate an idea before expressing a judgment.

11) **I have always followed the approach of over-delivering and over-servicing clients as a way to build and sustain an ongoing business relationship.** There is great satisfaction in completing a consulting assignment when you can provide your client with more than they asked for (within reasonable expectations), as it demonstrates a commitment to the client, which often will be the basis for

developing a long-term relationship and quality referrals of your company to others.

12) **I have learned the value of providing clients with written summaries of any decisions made in meetings.** People have short memories and sometimes remember only some of what was discussed in a meeting. As a result, it is a good consulting practice to confirm the details of any decisions made by sending emails, letters, or file memos to the client to confirm the agreements. While this requires extra time to do the writing, it will ensure that there is agreement about the interpretation of what was decided to avoid future problems due to the recollections of different people as to what was agreed to in the meeting.

13) **A successful consultant will never turn away business because they are too busy with other assignments.** This is a position that every consultant would like to be in, where they are so busy that they question whether they could possibly take on additional work. If the goal of the consulting practice is to grow, then the option of turning away a potentially good piece of business should not be considered. It is very difficult to develop a consulting business, and sometimes sacrifices must be made to complete the work that has been obtained. While I would never suggest sacrificing the quality of your work product to handle more business, I do feel there are some ways to approach the wonderful theoretical situation of having to decide whether you should take on more business at a time when you are swamped with work. There are a few excellent ways to address this situation. One is to commit to working dramatically more hours (weekends and/or evenings) to free up time for the extra work. Another is to be upfront with the client and try to negotiate a somewhat longer than normal due date, so you can begin the assignment at a lower workload and catch up when other

work you are doing is completed. A final way to address this type of situation is to have a relationship with another person in your area of expertise whom you could call on to help with the assignment while you still act as the key client contact.

Legal Lessons

1) **I have found that partnerships are an extremely difficult arrangement and infrequently work. They are particularly problematic when the arrangement is a 50/50 relationship.** It is my experience that the biggest issue with partnerships is the absence of a "boss," leader, or decision-maker in the organization. I have been involved with helping to solve many problems with partnerships among clients over the years and even experienced the issue myself during my consulting career. The absence of a designated "president" of the partnership makes the process of decision-making very difficult, as there are frequently no rules as to who is responsible for what areas of the business and who makes decisions regarding operations of the partnership. While virtually all partnerships begin with very good intentions, when the partnership is making a lot of money, problems with the arrangement are much less likely to occur. However, when the business is not making (enough) money, problems can occur relative to who is responsible for the decline in business. It does not matter whether the partnership is between two people or five. When things get tough, the basic issues of this type of relationship surface. For example, the biggest issue is generally the generation of revenues for the business. This is normally the first issue that becomes problematic as if the sales are not there (whether it is a product or a service business), there is no way to pay the bills and remunerate the partners.

In service businesses, in particular, the going-in expectation is that each of the partners will contribute equally relative to bringing in business for the company. However, this rarely is the situation. Some people are excellent salespeople but not particularly effective in project/engagement management, whereas others are outstanding at the management of an assignment but are not particularly effective when it comes to generating new business. As a result, "finger-pointing" can become a big issue that could damage or even destroy a partnership. If the partnership is formed where the percentage ownership is a separate issue from the decision making and the compensation, the organization has a much better chance of survival... particularly in difficult times.

2) **A major issue within partnerships is often related to the expenses incurred by the various partners.** Whether these are legitimate expenses incurred for the purpose of building the business or questionable expenses (i.e., travel, meals, etc.) that partners expense for tax purposes, there must be agreement as to the guidelines for addressing the handling of expenses. For example, legitimate business expenses should be immediately reimbursable. However, I have found that the best way to address the "questionable" expenses is for each partner to maintain a ledger of their questionable expenses. At the end of the year, these expenses should be deducted from the year-end compensation for each partner as a way to equalize this very important area and keep peace within the group.

3) **When working with an attorney, it is important to recognize that most legal issues are not "black and white."** For example, almost every legal question can be associated with a probability of it creating a problem. For example, if your attorney tells you that a phrase in a piece of advertising probably does not conform with the law, as a manager, you have to determine if it is worth taking the chance of going with the advertising, recognizing that you might have legal difficulties in the future. Your attorney's goal is to protect you from legal problems, and therefore most lawyers

are quite conservative, looking at the worst-case scenario. Therefore, I always find it important to weigh the risk of legal problems with the potential benefits of almost every legal recommendation before automatically changing what you had planned based on the lawyer's recommendation.

4) **One of the most important things that partners should recognize is that a very detailed *partnership agreement* is absolutely essential to protect all of the partners in an organization.** The goal of a partnership agreement should be to establish parameters of how the partnership should handle any event, such as a partner leaving the organization as a result of death, disability, or any other reason. The most important part of a partnership agreement is the section that provides the procedure that can fairly address what happens upon the departure of a partner. The two key issues in this type of situation are how much money should the departing partner receive (and over what time period) and what happens to the shares owned by this individual. A key to addressing these issues is what the value of the business is at the time of the partner's departure. Very few organizations spend the time to develop a formula for valuing a business when it is formed, and as a result, when they need this information, it can become both very confrontational and extremely expensive. I have worked with partnerships that have broken up effectively within a matter of hours (due to a well-written partnership agreement) and others that have taken years in court trying to figure out what the departed partner is entitled to after leaving the company.

In most partnerships agreements I have seen, the issue of a departed partner is almost never addressed, and there is rarely an attempt to develop a formula for valuing a business from start-up to maturity. To this end, I recommend a valuation formula be structured in modules, with the initial one being the first year of the business because the relevant financial issues at that time are the investments made by the partners, the business generated to date, and the potential value of the proposals that are outstanding. During the first year, it is unlikely that the entity has developed any equity value, which can be a major issue for an established organization.

The next module should consider years 2-5 of the partnership, as the value can be based on both the investments of the partners and the earnings performance in the initial years. After approximately five years, the equity in the name (i.e., awareness, reputation, etc.) can be significant and should be a major factor in the formula to value the partnership.

5) **There are many legal actions that can be implemented without an attorney, therefore saving considerable money for the organization.** While there are definite advantages to retaining an attorney to handle most legal issues, when considering matters such as setting up an LLC, an "S" Corporation, a non-profit 501c3, or even a "C" corporation, these can be done easily without an attorney. For example, establishing an LLC is a very simple procedure with almost no paperwork in all states but New York (which has different rules than the other 49, as discussed below). Most people could complete this task in under ½ hour, and as a result, the only fees involved are the registration costs to the state where the LLC is located. Another option that can save significant money is to use an organization such as LegalZoom.com rather than a private lawyer to execute many different types of legal matters. I have had many experiences with LegalZoom and have found them to be very efficient and much less expensive than hiring an attorney to handle simple matters

6) **The LLC (limited liability corporation) is an excellent corporate form that is very popular for small to medium-sized businesses.** However, if your business is located in New York State, there are some important decisions to be made that do not exist relative to LLCs in the other states. New York has different rules for LLCs that might make alternate corporate forms (i.e., "S" corporation) more beneficial. Therefore, it is essential to check with your accountant and/or lawyer before establishing an LLC.

7) **It is essential to obtain qualified legal counsel when you are involved in signing any non-compete agreements.** I am not an attorney and would never attempt to provide any type of legal advice, so what I am sharing is based on my own experience of having been involved in several situations regarding non-compete agreements. To this end, it is important to keep in mind a few key points I learned. First, "clients have rights." Therefore, I have found that a non-compete can stop you from soliciting specified clients, but if you don't solicit them and they come to you, it has been my experience that this may not be prohibited by a non-compete. A second area of the non-compete restrictions relates to how much you can be restricted and for what period of time. Specifically, the geographic area of restriction must be reasonable, and the time frame also must be fair. The net of this is that a non-compete generally cannot restrict you from ever operating in a particular business, but it does offer some protection to your former employer relative to your efforts to take away business that rightfully they feel is theirs. The net of all this is that it is important to work with a competent attorney before you sign a non-compete so you can minimize the restrictions on you once you separate.

Miscellaneous Lessons

1) **A picture is definitely worth 1000 words.** This is not new information to anyone, but when it relates to speeches and presentations, it is really true. If you are inclined to conduct workshops, seminars, or give speeches, I can guarantee your presentation will be dramatically more effective if you carefully use visuals to reinforce what you are saying. People learn much better, and their comprehension is significantly better when visuals are used in the presentation. This is not to suggest that you should put up every point of your presentation on a screen, but clearly showing visuals that reinforce the points you are making while speaking will increase the overall impact of what you are saying. One thing that must be kept in mind is that the "words and pictures must go together." In other words, be sure the visuals you show relate directly to what you are talking about. I also have found that presentations can be made much more effective by occasionally using a photo or clip art slide that will add some humor to the presentation.

2) **When giving a presentation, it is advisable NOT to hand out copies of your slides to the audience at the beginning**. While some people argue that having the slides in the beginning is a positive as they can take notes on them while you speak, I have always felt the opposite because (a) people tend to look at slides ahead of where you are, which affects their attention to what you are saying, and (b) it encourages them to take notes while you are talking—you want them to concentrate on what you are saying and not on writing copious notes.

3) **When conducting presentations using PowerPoint, I have learned there are very simple techniques you can use that will help the audience focus on what you are saying, which will improve the impact of your speech.** Specifically, when presenting a list of items you will be covering, use the capabilities of PowerPoint to present only one item at a time, and when you are finished with this item, bring up the next in the series but dim out the previous item. In this lesson, I strongly recommend that you do NOT show a complete list of items at the same time, as it is difficult to get your audience to focus on the specific one about which you are talking.

4) **A final lesson regarding PowerPoint presentations that I have always found helpful involves utilizing the built-in capabilities of the program to add interest and value to your talk.** Specifically, I am referring to the use of transitions between slides as it is very easy to add interesting variety to your transitions to help keep the audience engaged. Similarly, when you have multiple items/words/pictures on one page of the presentation, take advantage of the simple capabilities of the PowerPoint system to have items come in and out of the slide in an interesting way. This also adds interest value to the presentation. Effective use of the capabilities of a program such as PowerPoint can definitely make a good presentation significantly more effective.

5) **One lesson I learned in my 11 years as a volunteer counselor at SCORE is the value of utilizing outside resources (ideally free ones) to assist in starting or running a new OR existing business.** I often recommend to clients that they develop an advisory board of outside professionals who would volunteer time to meet with the business owner on a regular basis (i.e., quarterly, monthly, etc.) to ask questions and to provide objective advice and general guidance that would be helpful to the leader. This concept

is different from a paid Board of Directors as it has no authority but rather serves as a resource to help guide the growth of the business. There are two excellent sources for these types of advisors. One is an organization such as SCORE, which has a mission of providing free counseling to small to medium-sized businesses. While there are vast differences in the quality of the mentors within the vast SCORE system (about 13,000 mentors in 300+ offices), you can easily change mentors if you are not happy with the ones to whom you are assigned. A second excellent resource for guidance is individuals who have retired from a successful business career. Often people in this category are very anxious to get back into the "action" and would be delighted to act as an unpaid advisor.

6) **A key lesson I have learned is that everyone is not cut out to be an entrepreneur.** While owning your own business is often thought to be the American dream, it is important that people recognize that not everyone has the capabilities to be an entrepreneur. For example, a successful entrepreneur should be an individual who is self-driven, self-motivated, able to work independently without direction, is a risk-taker rather than a conservative businessperson, and is a natural leader who establishes aggressive goals and will do almost anything to achieve them. Further, I have found that some people just are not meant to work independently and would function much better in a group environment. An example of this was a client who left the corporate world to start her own consulting company. In a very short time, she became a very successful consultant when measured on the basis of fees received and trends in revenues. However, after two years of successful consulting, she told me how unhappy sole-entrepreneur life can be, and she made the decision to return to the corporate world... at a substantial reduction of income.

Where to From Here?

My objective in writing this book was to pass along various lessons that I have learned from a long career on both the client-side (Procter & Gamble, Arm & Hammer, U.S. Army Office of Management & Budget) and as a consultant to both very large and very small companies. I felt that others might benefit from my 50+ years' experience since I left Columbia Business School in 1966.

I have tried not to get "into the weeds" too much, as my goal was to focus on lessons I have learned over the years that made a real difference in my functioning both in the product management/marketing world and as a consultant to over 400 different companies. During the three months I have been working on this book, I continue to remember new lessons, and I am sure that after I finish this book, more will emerge. I hope to issue an update to this book in a couple of years with lots of new lessons.

Please feel free to contact me with any questions or comments. I look forward to hearing from you.

Thomas L. Greenbaum
Founder
Encore Strategic Business Consulting
530 East 72nd St. PH C
New York, NY 10021
Email: tom@encorestrategic.com

About the Author

TOM GREENBAUM has spent the bulk of his career in consulting, working with more than 1000 different clients in a wide variety of business categories. His early training was in the Paper Products Division at Procter & Gamble, and then as a Product Manager at Church & Dwight, introducing the Arm & Hammer Laundry Detergent to the USA.

His consulting career began in 1973 at Glendinning Associates, a marketing consulting company staffed almost exclusively with ex-Procter & Gamble sales or brand management personnel. After six years, he and four other colleagues left Glendinning and formed The Connecticut Consulting Group, which provided marketing, sales, and promotion consulting to Fortune 1000 clients. After nine years, the company was sold to what is now Publicis, where Tom spent four years consulting in marketing and marketing research before leaving to form Groups Plus Inc., a focus group moderating and consulting firm. After 15 years conducting almost 4000 focus groups, Tom retired from Groups Plus and joined SCORE (Service Corps for Retired Executives), where he spent 11 years as a volunteer, counseling with well over 700 small business entrepreneurs. In 2019 he returned to his roots and started Encore Strategic Business Consulting, where he currently is actively consulting to several medium-sized business clients.

Tom has authored seven other books covering *Focus Group Research, The Consultant's Manual: A Complete Guide to Building a Successful Consulting Practice,* and *You Can Do it: A Guide to Starting & Running A Small Business.*